FINDING THE EDGE

JIMMY ANDERSON

THE AUTOBIOGRAPHY

FINDING THE EDGE

WITH FELIX WHITE

BLINK

bringing you closer

First published in the UK by Blink Publishing
An imprint of The Zaffre Publishing Group
A Bonnier Books UK company
4th Floor, Victoria House,
Bloomsbury Square,
London, WC1B 4DA

Owned by Bonnier Books
Sveavägen 56, Stockholm, Sweden

Hardback – 9781785123511
Trade Paperback – 9781785123528
Ebook – 9781785123535
Audio Digital Download – 9781785123542

Designed by Envy Design Ltd
Printed and bound by Clays Ltd, Elcograf S.p.A.

5 7 9 10 8 6 4

Blink Publishing is an imprint of Bonnier Books UK
www.bonnierbooks.co.uk

CONTENTS

CHAPTER 1

THE DAY AFTER

14 July 2024, 8:32am

It's the first morning in 21 years I am waking up not as a Test cricketer. The first time as an adult I am opening my eyes as someone else, a person undiscovered, a purpose unknown, a future unwritten. The last thing I remember from my final day as an England international is the sun coming up while sitting in a chicken shop at 5:30am. Joe Root had held my gaze in the dressing room after play and said, 'I'm doing whatever you're doing tonight.' There was excuse after excuse to keep the evening going, to stay teammates until the new dawn forced it over. Cricket is good like that. It sticks people together in irreversible ways, even when it can no longer hold you in the same team any more. We drank in the dressing room, waving to the crowds stretched out of the outfield at Lord's. We played cricket again with our children when the crowds left. We returned to the hotel bar where my family and friends had kept the celebrations going. Still not content, we found a bar in Chelsea. Hungry and stretching the night out, we found a chicken shop.

They wouldn't let us in at first. Joe had to take them aside and explain the situation; that there needed to be an end that fitted all the road we had travelled, all the suffering and joys and endless brutal cricket, and hot wings here and now in this establishment was the only acceptable ending. I squinted at him during his negotiation with the staff, where he looked like he was borderline pleading as if it was some kind of dying wish of mine, imagining him to be saying that a table is all we need to make this 41-year-old fast bowler happy after decades of service. After some negotiation, they looked back up at him and over at me and, like some sort of death row meal, made an exception for us. We could have whatever we wanted. And that's how it ended – the 704 wickets, the 188 Test matches, the 170 registered injuries, the endless feuds with all those grizzled cricketers – sitting with Joe, eating hot wings, shielding our eyes as the sun came up.

There were 330 pints drunk that day in the England dressing room. I can remember my first, sitting next to Nasser Hussain as soon as that first Test was won. It had all begun in the very same place with him as my captain all those years ago, when I entered to find a room packed full of players I'd only ever seen on television. It ended with Nasser again, this time him holding a microphone, live on Sky Sports, my current teammates gathered around me in silence, waiting on every word. I looked around the room as we went on air and scanned my team, first Ben Stokes to my left, already getting through his first Guinness, then the others, some not even born when Nasser had first picked me. There was probably a total of about

40 years' difference between my first teammates and the ones in here now. I wouldn't dare even try to look it up. But Nasser, in this new capacity, decades thawed out from the man who watched my first over go for 17 runs and then reluctantly apologised for the field he set, sat there now visibly moved, his hands gently trembling as we conducted one last interview. I didn't want to let the cricket go, and somehow found myself telling him, 'I'm still gutted I dropped that catch, to be honest.' It had stuck for a second, in my left hand, like a fairy tale, and then bounced out, like real life.

I can remember my second pint too, walking out on to the balcony to see Lord's scattered with tens of thousands of people, all looking back up at us, waiting for a glimpse. I downed it in one. It was one of the biggest cheers I've ever received. To be fair, it was quick. Still, I can also just about recall when I nearly broke down back in the dressing room, as Ben told the group that the most important thing about me was that I was a good bloke. Joe presents me with a fielding mitt, given the amount of coaching drills I will be doing with them for the remainder of the summer. The rest of that evening, there are holes. I can just about re-find the tenth pint, when a woman flown in from Rome hand-delivered a guitar from Coldplay that had been on stage with them that same evening. It was that kind of day.

I'm having to almost physically force my eyelids open from the haze this morning. There is a text at the top of a long list of unread messages – it is from Mick Jagger. 'Hi, Jimmy,' it reads. 'I wanted to tell you how much you have given to me and my family watching you play for so long,' he says, 'and what an inspiration you've been to me to keep going.' No one's going to retire Mick Jagger, I think to myself, for a split second envious.

I am taking my daughter, Ruby, to play netball. The Test has finished early, only just stretching into a Saturday morning where it was full for my last ever hour of Test cricket at Lord's, the same place it had all started. But today, somewhat abruptly, I'm no longer the leader of the England attack, I'm a dad with a teenage daughter who needs to be taken to netball. When our taxi arrives, my head rumbling, half grateful for the excuse not to be dwelling on the empty space and given some parental purpose, I drop her off at the game. After her first match, I feel the need to find somewhere to be alone, somewhere I can lie down, to process all this for a second, to get back to some of those messages, to ease the banging going on inside my head – that would be a godsend.

I dart out as the game finishes, avoiding the gaze of several parents looking at me with slightly upturned smiles and inward-facing eyebrows. I escape around the back of the sports hall, looking for anywhere I can just be alone, somewhere quiet and unburdened. *What am I looking for?*, I begin to ask myself, because it feels like a cave, or a cell, even a hole in the ground to bury myself in would suffice. I realise, though, on turning the corner, exactly where it is I need to be. On sight, it appears to be a mirage. A totally abandoned cricket pitch. There is no one on the horizon, nothing in my peripheries, just a vacated expanse of cricket outfield and a distant hut for a pavilion. When I approach it, body aching and creaking its way over, I see a single bench hugging the boundary. It is a bench not unlike the one I would travel to in Burnley, lost and alone. I find it, at first sitting and then, enjoying the silence, thinking it to be some sort of half-life between yesterday and tomorrow, I stretch out and lie there, completely alone. If I can just get ten minutes' sleep here, that will be nice.

I don't know how long I've been there when I get tapped on the shoulder. A man is there, but I don't catch his face. He just says, as I come to, 'You missing it that much already?'

CHAPTER 2

THE MEETING

27 April 2024, 12:00pm

It suddenly strikes me that it is weird all three of them are going to be there. Stokes, McCullum *and* Key?

I am on the tram, on the way to what I think is a contract appraisal. I'm not driving because I'm going to see Burnley play away at Manchester United later that afternoon. I'm excited to not only be going to the game but to catch up with my mates after being on tour for a couple of months. It's not an unusual Saturday afternoon in waiting. I've had many like it before. Appraisal. Yes, I agree, wish we'd done a bit better in India, especially after winning that first Test. Yes, thank you, me too, I'm pretty happy with how I bowled. Yes, ready to go this summer, can't wait. See you then. Watch Burnley play with Gaz and Dave. A few drinks. Home. Same as usual. That's the plan.

We are meeting at the Dakota Hotel in Manchester. It is midday so it's quiet in there, an erring sense of a busy space vacated. A few staff usher bits to and from corners of the lobby with the morning rush now done. It's a trendy hotel, intentionally dimly lit for privacy, and the three of them are waiting in the corner at the end of the bar, lights low, caps over their faces.

As I walk towards them, it hits me cold. This isn't a team appraisal, is it? With each footstep towards the far side of the bar, each of their distinct silhouettes coming into view, the tram journey just gone is suddenly like a blissful past life, the outdoor sun sucked into a horizonless neon red darkness. They are all wearing sympathetic expressions on their faces when I reach them – half the kind you get when a relative has died and half the kind of someone who is worried you're going to go for them. They sit there, nursing coffees. I read the room, follow suit and order the same. Their body language, even out of the dim lights, is a sickening concoction of that awful, patronising sympathy no one wants and palpable, pre-emptive self-defence.

My brain is doing the maths and my heart is sinking as I go to shake their hands. I feel like Joe Pesci in *Goodfellas*, ushered into a room under the impression that I'm going to get made, only to be shot. You fuckers. They're going to tell me something I don't want to be told, aren't they? Something I've been swerving, darting, shapeshifting, bowling through for my whole life. It's chased me for so long. I have half begun to feel it might never get me. I almost allowed myself to daydream that, somehow, I might be the only exception to the rule. But here it is – the career reaper – dressed as McCullum, Stokes and Key in the Dakota Hotel bar at midday in Manchester. They wouldn't choose to do this in a public bar though, would they? Maybe I'm paranoid. Maybe it is an appraisal.

I haven't yet had time to lean on one eventuality or the other when the words come sharply, if reticently, out of McCullum's mouth. They are organised and rehearsed, sure and slow: 'We are looking to the future,' he says, as the sides of the room start to blur. 'We don't think you're going to make it to Australia in 18 months' time and we want to see who would be good for that series and have the time to work it out.' Oh, this isn't even going to be a negotiation. It isn't even a conversation, is it? I'm being *told*.

The last time England had tried to do this, it was a 45-second phone call from Andrew Strauss before the West Indies tour in early 2022. He had just said on the phone, incredibly bluntly and swiftly, 'There's no easy way to say this, but we're going in a different direction. We're giving younger players a go.' That was it. No further information. End of call. I didn't want to argue because my kids were in the car. I didn't mention it to them, I just drove them home, phoned Stuart Broad, who had been dropped too it turned out, and went to the gym. We took our combined 1,177 wickets and raged ourselves fitter. They called it a 'red ball reset'. It turned out the red ball reset needed resetting itself quite quickly and three months later we were back in. Strauss and I have never spoken about it since. I guess you'd rather be stabbed in the front than the back.

This time, it's different. It's both kinder and harsher, more sympathetic and more ruthless and, worst of all, nauseatingly final. Their faces are stretched, trying to read my reaction. All I have to say is 'OK'. I can only say 'OK' again and again. I must say it a thousand times. In each 'OK', it's as if I'm trying just to buy some time for myself, process something not processable, but all I can think is, 'Not here, surely? How could it all end like this, in the fucking Dakota Hotel in Manchester?'

At the end of the speech and the other side of all my dimly lit 'OKs', there's an option offered to me. 'You can say, I'm happy with 700 wickets and what I've achieved and bow out now, or you can play one last time.' McCullum says, 'We would be happy to give you that first Test match at Lord's and that be it.' One more game? My option is never to play cricket for England again or play one more time? When that first over at Lord's went for all those runs 22 years ago, I would have run through the streets like Charlie with the golden ticket and snapped your hand off for one more. When I bowled second change for Burnley Cricket Club, I would have had to endure laughter from everyone in my team for the offer of an actual Test match for England. Now it comes, after 187 games, approaching 40,000 balls, and eight wickets short of Shane Warne's wicket tally as some sort of gesture of consolation. That part is easy though. If it's a choice between playing and not playing cricket, I always choose playing. All I say is 'OK'. We finish our coffees and switch to beer. Everyone needs one.

The staff fly by around us, clearing up the drinks, as I make my excuses to go. There is no outside sense of a lifetime's work having to stop in the hushed conversation that surrounds me. No tangible evidence of all the wickets and heartache. I'm half expecting them to ask if I'm OK, but then I realise, it's just me that knows this. This news is mine alone. Maybe that's always happening in these places, public bars intentionally picked for difficult private news to be broken, the recipient unable to make any scene, before the people are spat back out into the world again. As I leave, back into the sunlight and on to the tram, the world outside appears completely different to how I last left it. I think they might be amazed at how well I've taken it, about how drama-less the whole thing has been. They might even be thinking I took it ominously well. I'm wondering the same. I guess it doesn't matter either way. I'm floating out of the hotel, back on the tram to Old Trafford, and I call my wife, Daniella. It's only her that can know for now, they say.

She's in Boots, with Ruby. She's stunned, angry, immediately full of all the injustices that had not occurred to me sitting there. She seems more incensed for having to receive the news in Boots. All the Christmases we've missed, all the girls' birthdays I have missed because of a commitment to the England cricket team, all that sacrifice and the first thing that she can think is that she has to hear it's all over while she's in Boots. She knows how grief can merge with the everyday, the sheer disorientation of it. In 2006, she had watched me spend six months out with a stress fracture of my back, unable to move, persuading me that I would be able to play cricket again. We'd got through that, worked it out, weighed up all options and chosen sacrifice again. She couldn't believe that nearly 20 years later it would be put to bed like this.

When I get to Old Trafford, I realise we have tickets in the Manchester United end. Brilliant. Fucking brilliant. I'm there for 90 minutes, head down, pretending not to support Burnley, working out what it will mean not to play cricket for England. When the crowd have dispersed and the outer web of friends in the bar have gone, I tell Gaz and Dave – two of my closest friends – that I think it might be over. The words fall out of my mouth, like I'm trying them out for size for the very first time. Gaz and Dave just stare, shocked, expressions of concern reflected back at me. The world is upside down. It's there that I suddenly realise, soon I will never hear that question again. The one that has chased me around for more than ten years. Sometimes I wonder whether anyone else on earth has been asked a question as many times. My least favourite part of any social interaction. The one that came with every passing stranger or interview or end of a dinner or drink. I hated that question. It's finally here. The R word.

When are you going to retire?

Now I'd trade in anything for another ten years of hearing this question.

You'll know, they all said. You'll just *know*. I read it. I was told it. I even saw it happen, year on year, decade on decade, in front of my own eyes, with each of my teammates. I've had 109 of them. They all had that moment, that feeling, and left the England dressing room one by one; some sad, some relieved, some broken in body, some broken in spirit, all grateful, none unscathed. I waited and waited to know too. At times, I wished for the same brutal epiphany that landed in their laps, just to make my own peace with it. They all knew and, in their own way, accepted that part of their lives was moving beyond them. The only thing *I* ever knew is that I wanted to play cricket; always and forever. I would joke to people that I would have to be carried from the field to say goodbye. Now, I wonder if it was a joke at all.

Maybe I needed to be told to stop. Maybe it's a good thing that someone else made that decision for me. At least, that's what I keep telling myself.

After all, who would *choose* to stop doing the only thing they were put on this earth to do?

Especially if they knew they still could.

CHAPTER 3

THE ANNOUNCEMENT

11 May 2024, 2:08pm

A month passes, maybe more. I have kept it to myself. Nobody knows but Daniella, Gaz and Dave still. They are still angry on my behalf. I am at Trent Bridge in Nottingham with Lancashire as they play a County Championship game and I am preparing for my 188th and last England game, a fate that no one yet knows about. The retirement question is still routine daily interaction as, in some sort of new dissonance, my inner world completely disassociates from the outside. I remember this feeling; it's like being at school. I'm alone with my own reality and no one to share it with. England media manager, Danny Reuben, phones me. There's an urgency in his voice, one laced with that same reticence, dread and self-protection as the tone in that bar. The news of the retirement has been leaked, he tells me. Ali Martin has heard about it and would like to call me. I get the call at 2:08pm. 'Jimmy, I've heard that Brendon McCullum has flown over from New Zealand to tell you that the Test team are looking to the future and you'll be playing your last game this summer. I'm sorry, but it's an unignorable story.' At the end of the tour, McCullum's answer to Martin's question on my chances of making the next Ashes suddenly flicks back into my mind. 'I don't know, honestly,' McCullum had said then, 'who knows where the end of the line for him is?' It's all starting to slowly fall into place. I understand, I tell Ali. We've known each other 15 years. This is his job. It's done swiftly, amicably, I just ask how long I have until the *Guardian* prints it. He texts me soon after, at 2:30pm, saying his office have said it will go out at 5pm. I have a few hours before it's going to be announced to tell whoever I need to tell.

So, that is when I break the news to my parents, my friends, a few teammates. I explain what's happened and that I have since gone back to ask whether I could play a Test at Old Trafford one last time, maybe play a few games through the summer and then happily go with everything achieved, and the powers that be have told me no. It's one Test or nothing. All those wickets. All that drama. All that pain. All that time, and this is how I'm telling the people closest to me; on my own, overlooking the car park in the lunch room at Trent Bridge. I call them, staring out at the bland, stacked nothingness of parked cars. I frame it in a way that sounds like I am comfortable about it. Underneath, something is rattling me about the way this is all going down. I'm behaving more at peace with it than I actually am to protect them, to dial down the volume of the injustice they might feel on my behalf. My dad sounds like he's taking a call for which he has been preparing himself for years. My mum is more emotional. I'm going to stay on with the coaching team, I say, but Lord's is the last Test and the news will be out at 5pm. I don't know how the papers got the information, I say when they inevitably ask. I'm not sure where the leak came from. As we talk, I realise how angry I am about not being able to do this in person with people who have travelled with me on this journey, that a fundamental courtesy has been overlooked. I couldn't tell most of the people I wanted to know about the news in time – there's not enough room in the afternoon to contact people as I semi-manically scroll up and down my contacts trying to think who needs to know. Then I give up. They will find out through the article and their phones at 5pm. It doesn't feel right, to be sitting here, out of control of anything, just waiting.

As the news breaks, I just sit there, watching it all become real. My phone is an endless newsreel of my own career ending. That evening, I am a few Guinness deep, speaking to friends, processing the unprocessable. I think of Greg James and *Tailenders*. Our show has been an escape from the seriousness of cricket for the last six or seven years, but maybe my first response could be in the safest place possible to me, where I know I will get the time and space to say it how I need to. I'm going to need some sort of statement too. An international career that has lasted 19 years, and I have not once planned what a retirement statement might look like. I text Greg, 'would you be able to help with what I write in the post?'. 'Of course,' he says. I write out a short and sharp example for him, paraphrasing what I am struggling to articulate: 'Lord's will be my last Test. Been an amazing 20 years. Couldn't have done it without the support of so many people. Mainly Daniella, Lola, Ruby, my mum and dad. Excited for the future. That's the gist'. The next morning, Greg has taken the gist and written me something to post out, and we record an 'emergency' *Tailenders*, where I say it how I want to say it. It's comforting, in its own way, but no less surreal, the words still not fitting me as they leave my mouth.

I don't know how it all feels yet. All I know is, I have two games left of cricket to play, one at Southport for Lancashire against Nottinghamshire, and then one at Lord's for England against the West Indies. Beyond that, everything is unknown.

CHAPTER 4

SOUTHPORT

30 June 2024, 4:05pm

LANCASHIRE vs NOTTINGHAMSHIRE,
County Championship, *Southport*

Lancashire 353/9 dec. / Nottinghamshire 126 & 270/4 dec.
(following on)

Match drawn

First innings: **J Anderson 16–3–35–7**

It's so cold. The kind of cold that makes you forget what you are doing, cuts off feeling from your toes. For two days, I've been hiding from it all in the dressing room. Only a few months ago, I was playing at the bottom of a mountain in Dharamshala in India, a cricket ground that had not been built when I started playing. The ground was flanked by white snow-capped mountains, lending a bizarre sense of foreboding to the occasion. I'd become locked in a battle with Shubman Gill during that Test. He'd just brought up his century and ran past me and told me it was time to retire. I got him out two balls later. I said nothing, just felt him watching me as he walked past.

Not long after, I'd taken my 700th Test wicket. Kuldeep Yadav. Being a bowler and not a new-era batting icon, he'd been more self-effacing about the whole thing and said to me before I took the wicket, 'I just know I'm going to be your 700th wicket, aren't I?' I smiled and half shrugged, half nodded. It was strange because people would constantly ask that too – when are you going to get 700? I didn't know. It didn't really work like that. I felt like telling them, 'I don't get to choose.' All I cared about was playing games of cricket, winning games of cricket for England. It's still disturbing to me there's only one more I'm being allowed to play. Regardless, it would be difficult to find a cricket ground in the world so far opposed to Dharamshala, where I had last played a competitive game.

Southport, by contrast, is dwarfed by surrounding houses, not mountains, with a few rows of deck chairs and school chairs distancing the streets to the pitch. There is though a strange frostiness here too. A coldness inside and out. There has been rain and constant interruptions and I am the only one of 22 players who hasn't even walked out on the pitch yet. It's disorientating as the little out ground is unusually packed. People have travelled from miles around to see the game. Everyone keeps asking me how everything *feels* – how it feels that people have turned up just to see me, how it feels to be the last time, how it feels for it to be over. If I knew, I'd say. All I want to do is play cricket, to be in that safe space of semi-red mist with someone like Shubman Gill, where everything is simpler.

It's even weird with my other nemeses from around the world, who are now suddenly acting like they don't hate me anymore. Nathan Lyon is in the Lancashire team and he's being really friendly. I can't work out if I like it or not, but end up signing him a shirt, writing, 'I preferred you as a teammate to an opponent. Jimmy x'. People surround the path to the dressing room with messages and ask for photographs. All I'm thinking, all I will be thinking at Lord's too, is how do I not turn this into a procession? How do I not make this entirely about me but instead a game of competitive cricket, where that is all that matters? That's all I ever wanted. As I'm running back to the tiny dressing room having faced two balls, finally ready to bowl with Lancashire declaring to try to force a result, I decide to stop thinking; stop it all, block out all the cold and all the noise, and just let myself slip into the familiar safety of bowling.

I know how I *feel* with a ball in my hand. I feel really good. I feel really young. Every ball I bowl, I feel like I am going to take a wicket. The ball is doing stuff off the pitch I'd forgotten about; zipping through, rushing players for time, splaying off top edges and outside edges. Batters are squaring up, imagining the ball to be flickable through midwicket before it straightens late and leaves them stranded and twisted up. I'm floating through it, no coldness in my toes, no retirement in my mind, and look up at the scoreboard. I've taken six wickets for 18 runs in nine overs. There is nothing telling me I am tired, no other feeling than being where I am meant to be.

The figures read 16–3–35–7 as I eventually walk off. I would have bowled all day. They were the best figures anyone had returned in the Championship all season. I couldn't help but think as I turned around to the applause of rows of deckchairs, should I be going? Does this make sense to me that I should be finishing? Either way, the spell has helped me somehow. It's softened me, just to know I'm not delusional, I'm still as good as I've ever been. I'm all the bowlers I've ever been. There's a message on my phone when I get back to the dressing room. It's from Ben Stokes.

'Did you really have to do that?'

'Sorry, mate,' I said.

CHAPTER 5

THE LAST DANCE –
DAY ONE

10 July 2024, 10:17am

ENGLAND vs WEST INDIES, 1st Test, *Lord's* – Day 1

West Indies 121 all out; England 189/3

'Enjoy every moment,' I'm telling Jamie Smith, born three years before my Test debut, 'because the end comes much quicker than you think.' Even this morning, it feels like time is slipping out of my hands, moving quicker than I can ever remember it moving. It all feels really rushed. No one mentions anything before the game. There are no speeches. No addresses for anyone to make. I don't want them to. I want to be inside a real Test match one more time, all focus on winning for England. I'm lacing up my boots in the same place I've sat in at Lord's for 15 years, gravity pulling me towards the centre of the room, when Ben Stokes takes a seat next to me. 'Do you know anything about what's happening this morning?' No, I tell him, apart from my girls ringing the bell on the balcony. 'Well, there's going to be a video and then you're going to lead us out on to the field.'

It's my worst nightmare – I don't tell him – to be lined up in the Long Room, next to the West Indies players, while a video plays out across the huge screens at Lord's. I am caught between the sadness of not being the centre of attention on the pitch imminently, that beautiful feeling of having the ball in my hand and knowing everything is within my control, and actually being the centre of attention now in a way that is deeply unsettling to me. I'm wrestling with it all; the present and the past, the warmth and the cold, the gratitude and the hurt, the spotlight and the shade, the life and the death. As we leave the dressing room to make our way down the famous stairwells of the home of cricket, I can hear them already. My spikes, out of the dressing room first, set off a harsh clashing of sounds as they ping against the echoing interior of the pavilion. This time, though, they do not clatter with the same endless delay. The sound is soaked up by the hum of people, the acoustics warmer, more rounded. The members are packed in at the bottom, already waiting, already applauding. They will be there, in the same fashion, every time I walk these stairs for the next few days, applauding and whooping loudly on sight every time I'm there. It is then that it occurs to me, just as it had as I walked in through the Harris Garden this morning, dropped off at Gate 6 as always, Joe Root next to me with a coffee as television cameras manically walked backwards to track our steps in – it doesn't actually even matter what happens here, does it? The victory has been won many times. I've already achieved everything I would have liked to, and more.

At the bottom of the stairs, I peer out, waiting for the

introduction that has been cued up. The sky is moody out there, almost mournful, with clouds hanging low against North London, setting a grey backdrop across the ground that, as I lean out of the Long Room to look out on to a field so familiar yet, today, so foreign. I can see that the place is almost full, and then hear that same voice I've been hearing here for years over the PA, the tinniness of the tannoy that's always slightly more piercing than you would like it to be, but now somehow twice as loud as it's ever been, bouncing across Lord's.

'Playing for England under his eighth prime minister,' it begins, as a multitude of different statistics and measurements of time via wickets and Test matches disappear into the air. I'm just standing there, half apologising to everyone with the look on my face. This is like the surprise birthday party I never wanted, blown up into some sort of collision with the end of *The Truman Show* as the narrator explains back my life to me through a storm. Then, there's the video; all I can catch, leaning out, is the sound of it, set against commentary and wickets over the years, the sound of stumps clattering again and again, repeated and repeated, edges of a ball being nicked, the softness of the ball landing inside a slip fielder's hands. All those sounds that marked something sweet, the only thing I've strived for, played out on repeat one last time in cinematic vision. It feels like everyone I've ever known is there too, watching back on slow-motion replay. Once we've got out there, the actual game approaching providing a sort of relief from the storm, we line up for the anthems, staring back at the pavilion. Up there, by the bell, are my whole family, looking back. Ruby and Lola take the bell, an arm each on it, rattling it with overawed faces, huge smiles, ringing that thing as hard as they can. That's the first time I feel it behind my eyes, the swell of emotion meeting the outside, the overwhelming feeling of all these things in my life colliding at once to signify an end.

Suck it in, I tell myself, and allow this to happen; it is magical to experience this. Not many will. Once upon a time I dreamed of being this person. Be him one more time before he has to go. Chris Woakes gives me a hug as it calms and as I reach the end of my run-up, waiting to bowl my first ball. I flash back for a moment to my debut, at this very same mark, on this same patch of grass. Then, I trembled with nerves, questioning whether I belonged. Here, I just breathe in, let go, remind myself what ball I'm going to bowl and set off.

I don't know if I'm just trying to make sense of it for myself, or if there is some kind of transition happening as I run through the quicksand of the first innings of the first Test, but I bowl well for not much reward and stand in the field, collar up, hands behind my back, while debutant Gus Atkinson rips through the West Indies with record figures on a debut, finishing with figures of 12–5–45–7. He has a photo of us together when he is young and tells Sky later how surreal it felt for him to be standing next to me, watching me bowl.

For the first time in months, my nervous system registers it all. The months of waiting – the meeting in that public bar, the scurried messages overlooking that car park. It feels like, as much as the decades of bowling, they have loaded some sort of heaviness in me now too. I can feel the body catching up with me. I am running in as fast as I can, unleashing with what feels like the same venom and whip and intent as my prodigal years, only to look up and see the speed gun read just 79 mph. My ankle's as sore as it's ever been. The spurs that broke off years ago are pinching every time I land in the crater, reminding me of my age, telling me that the years have not been without cost and my body, with the adrenaline of a series no longer in front of me, starts to show its hurt.

CHAPTER 6

THE LAST DANCE – DAY TWO

11 July 2024, 11:00am

ENGLAND vs WEST INDIES, 1st Test, Lord's – Day 2

West Indies 121 & 79/6; England 371

In the second innings, with the initial fuss dispersed, something clicks. This morning, I have really enjoyed myself. Like at Southport, it's as if I've suddenly been able to re-access all the balls from the past, every different me that has bowled for England, all the different skills and separate evolutions inside me, ready to be called upon with every ball I choose to bowl.

The ball is not swinging at first, so when faced with Kraigg Brathwaite, I know I have to try to do something off the pitch first to keep him honest. I'm moving the ball off the seam, up the famous slope, concentrating on a certain area, allowing him to watch it move. Brathwaite is a stubborn, disciplined cricketer, so I know again I must be patient and wait. The lacquer starts to come off the ball and it starts to swing a little, just a tiny bit, giving him something to think about. With both seam and swing now in his mind, I hold the shiny side of the ball to move like an inswinger but grip the ball as a wobble seam delivery. He tries to track the ball, but with the seam scrambled, it's harder for him to read. It swings towards him, tracing in and spearing itself at him, before then nipping back sharply to bowl him, down the slope, through the gate between bat and pad. My 702nd Test wicket is a carbon copy of my 500th. That one was Brathwaite too.

There was another too. Alick Athanaze has shown courage and discipline for the West Indies and, grinding my teeth and relishing the call to arms to seduce a Test batter into doing something they are telling themselves not to do, I bowl patiently at him. I can see that he wants to be very deliberate with what he plays at, what he leaves and to not unnecessarily go at anything. I love this type of battle. I know this one well. I bowl dead straight at him for a few overs, getting him into the habit of having to play every ball, each giving him no option but to block and be watchful. Then, when I sense he has been lured into the habit, I approach the wicket slightly wider, giving myself a wider angle, hanging the ball a fraction outside the off stump, marginally fuller and from a slightly different trajectory, so it appears to be a blessed final run-scoring delivery. His eyes light up. This is the run-scoring shot, he decides. He drives. Outside edge. Jamie Smith catches it. As he does, I reel back to the hundreds of identical wickets I've taken.

I've taken 123 wickets at Lord's, and there is a little of each of them in both those balls.

CHAPTER 7

THE LAST DANCE – DAY THREE

12 July 2024, 11:26am

ENGLAND vs WEST INDIES, 1st Test, Lord's – Day 3

England 371; West Indies 121 & 136

England won by an innings and 114 runs

On the third morning, there is only a maximum of an hour of cricket likely to be played, for which the result is a total foregone conclusion. We've won the game by a distance. Normally, this would mean empty crowds on the final day, there being no reason to get in. Today, my final day for England, there's not an empty seat anywhere in the ground. People rush in manically from the outside, needing to be there for the opening moments. I walk out for the last time, through that dressing room, down those stairwells, to be met by a guard of honour in front of me. I'm semi-sheepish still to be receiving it and walk through feeling quite shy about the whole thing. It doesn't temper the sense of strange occasion though and where two days earlier I had felt heavier, loaded with expectation and lucklessness, today there is a sense of true alignment. From the very first ball, I am swinging it at will. It is going around corners, almost playfully. Joe Root keeps checking the ball, confused, it being in bad shape. 'It's so weird,' he tells me. 'It looks like a dog chewed this. I've never seen a ball like it swing.' We will decide later in the chicken shop that it is divine intervention, but for now, I don't think and just bowl.

I'm bowling at the Nursery End and the ball is swinging. It's the best feeling in the world. Josh Da Silva waits. I know what ball I'm going to bowl. I've visualised it all the night before. It's the magic ball. The one that swings away late, at first provoking the batter to whip it towards midwicket before straightening dramatically and leaving them squared up, the ball somehow finding the outside edge. I bowled it to Brendon McCullum in 2008, shattering his stumps. Strange how things end up. Ben Stokes comes up to me to from mid-off. I nod. He nods back. As I walk back to the start of my mark, I analyse the last ball. It's all the same questions I've always asked myself. Did it land where I wanted it to? Did it do anything in the air or off the pitch? What did Da Silva do? Did he play at a ball he didn't need to? Do I need to bowl the same ball again or do I need to do something different? Do I need to change the field? It all moves through my mind in 20 seconds; a quick-fire checklist of internal questions. Then I'm at the top of my mark again. Waiting. I've decided. I'm going to bowl that perfect delivery, the one that I throw almost down the leg side and then it shapes – I got the other two ticked off yesterday, so this one would complete the package.

I turn to receive the ball. There is a song in my head as it travels towards me. It's a mantra that briefly appears before disappearing again, reminding me the thinking part is done now, reassuring me that I'm relaxed. The ball is in my hand, where it belongs. It is comfortable. It's how I know everything is where it's meant to be, when I feel the ball with the tips of my fingers. The tips are where all the feeling is. I toss the ball twice out of my hand, re-finding the sensation each time as it lands, reminding the body of what it should feel like when the moment matters. Every time it leaves, it's as if it's on an imaginary string, a wire from the palm of my hand to the centre of its gravity, pulling it back to where I control it. I turn it in my hand as it settles. When it finds its resting place at last, the rope of the ball is rubbing against my index finger, where a callus now lives. The callus is the point at the top of my finger which would once blister as the ball brushed past it, causing repeated, quick, sliced, momentary friction. It has worn hardened and tight and resistant to pressure since. It marks time; all 40,000 of the balls I've bowled for England over 20 years have passed the same, tiny spot. When I feel the ball on it, the specific sensation of that small irritation, the familiarity of a feeling that is mine alone, that's when I know. I'm ready. A few overs ago, I've seen a big screen television replay of Lola jumping out of her seat when I've missed Da Silva's outside edge. This one is for her, I think. She'll like this one.

I hold my breath. It's as if I'm going under water. In seconds, I will resurface, again breaking the wall of conscience. I take off on my left foot, on the balls of my feet, in a momentary image of a sprinter just out of their mark. I've played the same game this morning before play as I have done for every one of the

21 years as an England player, guessing where the run-up is before measuring it out, marking the guess down in paint. I haven't guessed it wrong for years. The left foot hits the marker I've laid out as I take off, spray paint underneath it. I mark it out as 15 paces, 1 jump at the start and 1 jump at the end as I pace it out – the exact measurement is 15.5 meters. Everything is in synchrony: the run, the past, the present and the future.

I begin to run in, and the feeling off the marker is like a springboard. I'm accelerating and, as I do, I'm close to a trance. I know I'm in good flow because it feels like I'm gliding. There is no conscious effort anywhere. I have had days where I've approached the crease and felt out of breath, where every step is a chore, but today it's not taking anything out of me whatsoever. Someone has told me this week that if you collate every time I've done this back to back, I would be running in uninterrupted for 18 and a half days non-stop for England. Today, in this moment, I feel like I could do it all again. I'd be running in until no one is in the ground any more, just watching the ball do what it does.

I become weightless, floating, my feet and knees unburdened by any impact with the ground. Everything outside becomes meaningless. There is no one else inside the moment. Only me and the ball. The thoughts; all the processing, all the information, the chatter in the background, my teammates, my opponents, the objectives, the history, the future, the success, the failures, the score, it all evaporates. They are an echo of something unnecessary. I am nothing but a combination of pure forward motion and stillness. Josh Da Silva is in my periphery; a blurry, flinching distance which is getting closer and closer.

I have a sense of him, but that is all. I'm focusing on tempo only. I'm trying to swing the ball, so I'm not running in as fast as I once would have – it's all control, rhythm and tempo.

As I begin to reach the wicket, I become aware that I've been concentrating on the approaching crease. It comes into focus quickly and as it does, almost like a set of auto-pilot instructions with a pre-determined destination dialled in, I begin the delivery stride. Umpires will say to me, when everything is clicking like it is today, that they can't hear me running in, that they are only guessing at when I am arriving, as if there is nothing there. This is one of those times, where my run-up leaves no trace. The last step before the wicket, I am landing again on my left foot, this time turning almost completely side on, followed by a skip to take flight.

As I'm waiting to land on my right foot, just beyond the waiting umpire who stands stationary next to me, a kind of immovable waxwork point of reference, it all happens. I am coiled as a spring, left knee is in flight, bent and reaching my chest. I can see the wristband on my left hand move past my nose; in the early years it was a watch and now it's a white band. It shows me where the target is, allowing me to line up my right arm as it follows, joining the ball and that callus with the ball in the hand. The ball is not held tight. I can feel how loose it is for a moment, totally relaxed, almost like I could let it go and drop it, before it unwinds out of the coil, something rhythmical with it, the closest I will ever get to dancing.

As I land to deliver the ball, my right foot first lands at the same, strange angle it always has. They tried to re-model my action in 2004 to make it safer, but I decided to veto it after my stress fracture in 2006, going back to what I know, to all the natural idiosyncrasies. It's only on landing here that I re-feel my body and all the pain and history of damage. The spur, for example, that sticks out at the back of my right ankle as it does, the one that broke into quite a few little pieces and that I have had injected with steroids to ease the inflammation ever since. Then, as I reach to deliver, I recall in muscle memory the South African tour where I landed with such intensity, so often, that the muscle tugged at the rib until it snapped and broke a rib. As my arm goes over, I remember the time I had dived for a ball and landed on my armpit, jarring the shoulder. The broken fingers, the multiple calf tears, the groin that kept me out of an entire Ashes series. They are all there as I land, the memory of each of them. No England cricketer has ever had more injury records, the physio tells me.

As I let go, the ball shapes exactly where I want it to go. The magic ball. It travels towards the leg stump, causing Josh Da Silva to motion to hit it square, just like McCullum did, before doing the impossible thing that I have almost awed myself with over the years, straightening dramatically and catching the outside edge, Da Silva turned inside out.

Then it's all there again. The softness of the sound of the ball hitting wicketkeeper gloves. The teammates, the crowd, the sense of an outside world watching. I'm the centre of it, for one last time. At the end of the game, Josh Da Silva is walking past me: 'That was a privilege,' he says, 'to get out to you like that.'

As I turn to say goodbye, raising my hat and waving for the last time, it suddenly occurs to me how much time I have spent at Lord's. That, incredibly, for someone from Burnley, someone who found this place so distant and daunting and overawing, it feels like a home to me now. I would usually walk off as quickly as I could, just to get away from it all, back to the safety of the dressing room. This time, just this once, I take it all in and turn 360 degrees, waving, seeing a lifetime in the stands.

The crowd are still there when Mike Atherton interviews me back over the ground PA, another clipped up 'This Is Your Life' just having played out. 'You've got to have a sadistic side to be a fast bowler,' I remember telling him, 'because it does hurt. I won't miss getting out of bed and not being able to sit on the toilet first thing in the morning or lift my arms to brush my teeth.' I hear the laughter of 31,000 people and don't have the energy to tell them this isn't a joke. 'Test cricket is the perfect game,' I tell Athers. 'It shows you how much you've got inside you and how deep you can actually dig.' And what about Gus Atkinson's debut after record figures?, he prompts. I smile, 'I will say, it's downhill from here.'

The interview, the wickets and the walk off are not my abiding memories when I'm waking up on that bench, trying to put the rest of the night together, working out what to answer this stranger who's asking me if I miss it that much already. I just remember, with a new kind of profound satisfaction, chasing the ball to the boundary on that third morning, trying to stop a four that would have been completely inconsequential to the game. I was determined to catch it, running down the slope at Lord's and as I did, throwing my cap off in a final chase of sudden abandon, I remembered how I fell in love with cricket, where it all began; not with the bat or the ball, but just the pure joy of throwing yourself at a ball for your team in the field, even to save one meaningless run.

CHAPTER 8

THE HILL AND THE HAM SANDWICH

My mum drops me off at the entrance to Thompson Park. It's a two-minute walk into school through the gates, past the green bandstand that I will one day congregate under to smoke in the rain. I walk into the park, stopping just short of the bandstand, and watch her drive off into the distance. She knows that I'm not happy at St Theodore's, that I don't want to be going in. I wonder as I watch the car leave whether she even knows that I haven't been getting close to those school gates this week; that we maybe have an unsaid understanding that I don't need to if it's making me that unhappy. I've told her parts of what's going on; that I don't have any friends, that I'm getting picked on. She can see that I'm half the size of everyone I'm in a sports team with. She might even be able to sense that I'm not as good at sports as I prayed I might be when I was younger. She might notice that in social situations I've begun to bite my own tongue out of nerves.

But she doesn't know all of it. She doesn't know that when you are this age, you begin to believe what they are saying to you. That I've begun to believe I really am that small. She doesn't know that last week I was sat on the field with a few of them and, when I disagreed with what one of the boys said, he chased me around, eventually catching me, wrestling me to the floor, pinning me to the ground and rubbing his half-eaten Cornish pasty into my face until I surrender and all that is surrounding me as he does, the pack swarming as it happens, is laughter. She doesn't know that the blood covered across my England football tracksuit is not me hitting my nose on a pole, but from a headbutt, so sharp and direct and blinding that it rushed immediately across my face, painting the top red. She doesn't know that I go to sleep every night wanting to be someone else. I don't want to put that on her, or anyone else. I don't know where it comes from, and it isn't her fault. It isn't anyone's fault. I just keep this feeling inside me; that I am not who I want to be.

A minute later, as she disappears, past the opticians that my dad runs and will still be running 25 years on, I turn around and walk back through the same park gates, in the opposite direction to her. I walk away from the school, up the road, a jacket zipped up over my uniform. The only purpose to begin with is to get as far as I can from it. I walk past the road my dad will teach me to drive on in two years' time. Up that road is where my grandad lives, where me and my cousin play cricket. He tells me to give him the strike while he hits sixes, and I oblige. Right next to it lies my nana's on Deepdale Drive, where the whole family go around on a Sunday night to have potato pie. I turn around again to double-check my mum is gone, and that no one from school has spotted me. Luckily, Sarah, my sister, doesn't know about this either, she goes to school on the other side of town. She's much more sensible, much more together than me, almost like a third parent, only reluctantly coming outside to play cricket with me with constant persuasion. Nobody knows, least of all me, that the road I look back on, where other parents park and let their children out for school, will one day be pitched to me as being renamed James Anderson Way, and that I will refuse to let them do that.

Burnley is dug in like a valley; a sudden, scooped freefall in the surrounding countryside, swallowing itself into entrenched, tightly packed roads, defunct cotton mills and close, community life. Only 90,000 of us call it home. It tests you to leave it. It almost dares you to try. The roads get ever steeper as you leave, at first suggesting and then insisting that you come back to where you came from. I walk past Burnley General Hospital, where I was born in scorching heat on 30 July 1982. I weighed nine and a half pounds on that day, my parents' second child, pushing myself up in my cot at three days old and turning my head to the opposite side. I didn't sleep much for two years, apparently, and was very alert. At seven months old, I was back in the same hospital, suffering with metatarsus adductus, where the front part of my foot curved inwards. A plaster cast was on until my first birthday but, as my mum tells me, it didn't stop me crawling around and getting about. I turn to walk up Torquay Avenue, beginning the climb that leads the way out of my town. I walk past the church I will be forced to sing at a funeral in, packed into pews and reciting 'Tears In Heaven' for someone I only vaguely knew. Next to it runs the creek, its current always flowing the same way.

All I can think is to walk past it, against the tide, get beyond it, away from all of it, and keep going uphill. Uphill will lead me out, no matter how tired I get. Uphill is out. Uphill is free. That is my only bread trail.

As I am walking through Torquay Avenue, I allow for the gentle incline to help me saunter beyond the neighbourhood of detached houses. I know these from the occasional drives out of Burnley, where me and my sister sit in the back and argue about the lyrics to Belinda Carlisle or Cyndi Lauper or Kate Bush or Tears for Fears tapes our parents are playing in the front. The houses are humble still, the ones we pause mid-argument to scan as we drive through, but far bigger than my 1960s semi-detached.

Then I am up Sutton Avenue, strides getting longer as I feel myself drifting out of a sadness and into more of a daydreamy solitude. I am not skiving the way I have seen it advertised. The other boys choose to do it in pool halls, smoking and drinking in groups through the day before getting hauled in; their playful, rebellious plea for attention duly noticed and landing them back at school with toothy, proud grins the same afternoon. My withdrawal is less animated, far more private. I don't want to put it on anyone, to make a show, to let anyone down. I just need to be alone. After all, the truth is I don't have anyone that would want to do this with me even if I wanted. Somehow, it feels correct to make a point of this loneliness on a pilgrimage; to justify it to myself and align how it feels inside with how I find myself outside. To be alone, inside and out.

I'm no stranger to silence. I am doing the walk as quietly as I sat in school with a broken wrist caused by a fall on black ice that dropped across Burnley two years previously. I had slipped, football bag in hand, and put my hand out to break my fall as I did. Everyone had seen it on the way to school and yet, I just picked myself up and walked on. I told no one, I just sat in class, holding it, my jaws clenched tight, until a teacher told me I looked paler than the freshly painted white wall. 'You're really sweating,' she said, alarmed, before calling my mum to take me to hospital. When I got there, it was full of people who had been taken the same way by the black ice, and still the inner humiliation did not fade. I do the walk as quietly as the time I drop a catch for Burnley CC against Burnley FC in not even two years from now. I'm on the boundary and I spill the match-deciding chance, the ball trickling over the rope for six to lose the game. Feeling the cursed embarrassment and pain reserved for cricket alone, I do not tell anyone that my thumb is burning and burning then either, until Cathy Pickup, my teammate's mum, notices and, wine glass in hand, takes me to A&E, where they tell me it's badly broken. I do all these things in silence – I keep all these events in. I would rather sit there, in deep discomfort, than let anyone know any of it. Sometimes I think if I was shot, I would prefer to just bite my tongue.

I was hoping the Spar shop would be open and am relieved when it is – I have more than two pounds. I've saved the money from the Turkish Delight and cigarettes I usually buy outside the school newsagent every day amassing more of the loose change. I'm saving up long term for better football boots and batting gloves, but I'll have to dive into the savings today. I buy a ham sandwich and crisps at the till. The woman receives them, looks me in the eyes, for a moment scanning my face, before nodding. I gulp and nod back, taking from the look on her face that my eyes must be wider than I realised. She hands me my change. I wonder whether she too understands, like my mum, that I am doing something I need to do, and duly turns a blind eye. In her silence, I register her compliance and keep walking, against the tide, up the hill, out of Burnley.

I follow the signs for Heptonstall. I've never been to Heptonstall. I don't even know what Heptonstall is. All I know is that it takes me out; the signs leading there, and the steady inclination of the hill are my only compass. That way out. I'm walking beyond the Baptist Church, a huge sign reading 'Jesus is the only way', pointing towards the church and then also up the hill. I don't even glance at it. I keep walking. In this moment, I am leaving behind everything in my world. Smackwater Jacks, where I will drink jugs of Illusion cocktails on Friday nights in two years, Panama Joe's down the road, the Mortimers' house, my sister's school on the other side of town, all my relatives' and family friends' homes all within five minutes' walking distance of each other. I am leaving behind Burnley Cricket Club too, and with it the football team, whose ground backs directly on to the cricket club.

In Burnley, the background always bleeds into focus eventually. Walking out of the town centre and lifting myself out of the urban valley, the houses start to become made of the same stone that the walls are made of. The countryside that sits above and outside it begins to show on the architecture, little clues of what's outside, further up the hill, the difference blurring between nature and nurture. It becomes more indistinguishable, the power balance shifting as I reach further. It's like an arm wrestle, one slowly giving away to another. I am winning when everything is hurting but I am still gaining ground, carrying my burden uphill alone. There are no longer any paths marking my way. I am just on the road, occasionally blending into the shrubs to make way when a car goes past.

I know when I have reached it. I'm kicked with giddiness, as if I've happened upon the edge of the universe, for a moment unbalanced and teetering on something else. It's like I'm mainlining some other truth, some other possibility. I turn around, to see how far I have come. I am blissfully and completely alone. I check my watch. I've been walking for three hours uninterrupted. There is nothing but sheep and an old road sign. Heptonstall is another nine and a quarter miles. I don't have time to get there. I do, though, have time to sit here for a moment.

In front of the stone wall, on Robin House Lane, there is a gentle T-junction, the third option being a left to Colne, and a bench raised by wild growth. I clamber this final, small hilly increase towards the bench and, on sitting on it, notice it looks back on the entire stretch of Burnley. I take in the sight – an entire overview of where I live. It's my whole world, my past and my future. It could be this and holidays to Skipton to eat cheese toasties forever. From here, my school is just a dot amongst many dots, as inconsequential as the shooting stars that sometimes flicker across the northern sky. There's nothing keeping me in Burnley, apart from my family, I think to myself. I think of the careers advisor who has recently come in to talk to us and, when I said I'd like to play sport, they sarcastically spat back at me: 'Oh, you must be good then,' and laughed. Maybe she's right. After all, has anyone come from Burnley that I've seen playing sport on television? There was a gymnast once, I'm told, and Mark Harvey played for Lancashire and drove back into town with a Peugeot 206 with his name on it, but that's as many as I know.

It's peaceful here, on the outside of it all. *I wish I could be someone else*, I think to myself again. I want to be someone who isn't such an easy target, someone who isn't so small. I think it again and again until it becomes its own sort of mantra. I wish I could be somewhere else, a place where my shyness and awkwardness were inverted and sucked out of my system, where I could instead channel this kind of calm. Up here, it doesn't sound disturbing to want that. I'm not beating myself up for hoping to be this other person or for wishing to have more than I do here. I'm just accepting that this lives within me, the dream of an alternative life, stirring inside, looking for something to hook its claws into. I look over to the cotton mills and Turf Moor and the schools and the cricket club and then sense the comparative stillness here, only very occasionally broken by the shuffling of sheep and the stroking of the wind and feel, with a longing thrill, like maybe there is more outside of this. More meaning. Someone else I could be, someone other than *James Anderson*. If I found that thing, I'd cling to it for all it was worth; I'd try to never let it go. I eat the ham sandwich and crisps. I check my watch: three hours until school is over. I'd better get back. I'll be here again tomorrow. I'll miss it until then.

CHAPTER 9

HEROES

6 July 1986

I am four years old. He's been on the television all summer. There's something about the way he plays the game, something that he is articulating to me through the television, that has left a thunderbolt of an impression on me. When he serves, he throws the ball into the sky, and for a second, it is as if time suspends. He is poised and coiled, left arm reaching towards the sky, the ball still connected to his palm by some invisible force, both knees bent, before he rotates through the ball and his racquet unleashes as if all the time before it has been held and then released, spinning to catch up with itself. He seems slightly sheepish, self-effacing even, but when the ball is in motion and as soon as play is active, there is a calm. When the absolute centre of attention, it's like he is suddenly in total control, his every move so graceful and athletic. He is also throwing himself on the floor often, and people are applauding him for it. It's quite appealing. By the time he reaches the final of Wimbledon, I want nothing else than to be Boris Becker.

Becker plays Ivan Lendl at the centre of the global tennis calendar year, all eyes on him. There are no phones, no distractions. On days like this, it feels as if not only the whole of Burnley has quietened, everyone watching it, but the world outside too. Despite this pressure, he appears that day on television with an effortlessness that suggests it's just play to him, something that comes innately. By the end of his straight sets win, I have reorganised the living room as a vision of Centre Court. The settee is the net and after I watch every point, I recreate it exactly with the plastic racquet and soft balls I've been given by my parents – they do less damage and make less noise. If this means throwing myself on to the wooden floor for a diving serve and volley, landing face down and then springing back to respond when Lendl's return shimmies off the net in the final serve-breaking game, I do so without hesitation. There is no wall, no alley, no room that cannot be turned into a sporting arena, nowhere that I am unable to daydream what it must be like to be Boris Becker. He is my first superhero, his supernatural status confirmed to me when the lad next door insisted on playing Spider-Man and Batman around the outside of the houses and ended up flying through the glass of the front porch. I looked at him, splayed out in the mess, face up in his Spider-Man costume, and decided Boris was a better bet.

Sport is the only thing that ever holds my attention, the only thing that I want to be doing. Nothing else comes remotely close. My mum's earliest memories of me sitting still are in front of the snooker, watching a black-and-white TV that my grandad had. It transfixes me. It's like a puzzle to solve, but one

I somehow understand the principles of and rules to without needing them explained. I am not just looking at it, I can *see* it. I can see things before they happen; pitfalls and traps and sequences play out in front of me and I can remember them very quickly, scoop up all the information without any excess thought. There's one player – there's always one specifically from each sport – that I feel closely affiliated with. Steve Davis is assured and omnipotent, ruling the landscape of snooker on TV. He, like Becker, has some sort of tangible connection to the sport he plays. The game somehow *is* him. Every time he plays, the world is airbrushed with an unfussiness and a simplicity that evades me in my life. He also has a look on his face – an acquired, knowing humour, a dry wit. It's like he's having a conversation with himself, making a joke that only he has heard. I like that about him. My cousin and I play snooker on the half-sized table at my grandparents', where I practise that knowing look, the smirk that lurks behind the seriousness of it all, while wandering around the table with deadly purpose.

Even before Boris Becker introduced me to high-risk indoor re-enactment or Steve Davis taught me layered and unreachable knowing, I was being channelled into sport. At Christmas, my uncle would take me upstairs at my grandparents' and set the dartboard up on the floor, when I was still barely able to walk, ensuring I could get eyeline with it, propped up against the bed, to throw darts. It came naturally to me, to repeat the action again and again, aiming to land the dart in the exact same spot, the noise of outside blocked out and hushed while I set myself a target to throw at. Eric Bristow – the rule-breaking star of darts in the 1980s – was another one of my heroes when I grew old enough to watch it on the telly and understand what was going on. There was something transformational about Bristow. He looked like all my parents' friends and almost every other adult male in Burnley – there was nothing about him that remotely resembled a high-level athlete. Watching him in the living room had the disorientating effect of feeling like he was sitting next to you, watching the darts too. And yet, when he stood in front of a dartboard, he transformed. The little finger of his right hand pointed out as he threw, a tiny sleight of hand that separated him from his opponents. He twiddled the dart. There is no other word for it. He twiddled it. The darts rotated and speared out of his hand, landing on the board with an energy and a fizz unimaginable to anyone he shared a board with. And then he was back again, drinking beer and smoking and watching the darts with everyone else.

And where each of these heroes had some sort of specified, designed relationship with their sport, Daley Thompson had decided he could do all of it. At the 1988 Olympics, participating in the decathlon, he was like an action figure from my wildest dreams. He was doing everything I was doing, just at a slightly higher level. He ran 100-metre sprints, he did hurdles, he jumped into sandpits, he jumped over impossibly high bars, he threw javelins and what appeared to be boulders and tiny little UFOs through the sky and into the distance. There was nothing he could not do, he was a natural at everything. Broad-shouldered, he was the definition of smouldering. He did not even need to say anything. He said it all when he competed.

I remember the commentary during his pole-vaulting heroics at the LA Olympics in 1984. It must have filtered into my system because I can recall the commentator saying, 'He hasn't been beaten since 1978, and when he did then, he cried for two days.'

I would have been halfway through turning the living room into a pole vault arena when I heard it. It is quite hard to imagine Daley Thompson alone, crying for two days, but I somehow already knew his pain. His sacrifice was all there, in those shoulders, the way he had to stay tall at all times, as if one chink in the body armour and he would buckle under the invisible pressure he was holding up. There was some sort of solace to knowing the cost, and that losing hurt Daley that much too. Because, even then, I was finding it hard to articulate to myself how much it hurt me to lose. It hurt so deeply, in so many ways, even in the most meaningless situations.

I was well trained in losing too. My dad loved to compete and he never let me win at anything. I would come home from playing him at any sport and my mum would instantly know who had won and who had lost. We would be wearing it. My mum, not often moved to big displays of emotion, once threw a Monopoly board at him because he was being a 'smug winner'. I made sure to make note, and try not to be a smug winner myself, because I knew how much losing hurt and how, even in a game of backyard football, or marbles, or a quiz, or Kwik Cricket, it found a place inside you, hollowed you out. I never needed anyone else to push it further down my throat.

Wildly inspired by Daley, I also reimagined the living room as the 110 metres hurdles, when tennis season was over, the track running around the settee and cardboard boxes fashioned as hurdles. My mum thought they were too high, that I was going to fall. I was fine, I told her, and sent her upstairs. She heard the thud seconds later and, face down, I had to admit defeat; I knew she'd heard it. 'You were right, Mum,' I shouted up the stairs, hearing back the sound of exaggerated rolling eyes.

Daley probably had to suffer like that too once upon a time. But Mum had to determine where to draw the line between standing in my way and leaving me in danger. She had watched me, after all, even at two years old, turn down a bucket and spade for a ball to kick and throw on holiday in Wales. She knew she had no choice. She didn't, however, take as kindly the next day, and drew the line further when she saw me using her garden laundry poles as javelins in the road outside.

At night, when she was reading to me to get me to sleep or talking me down from whatever activity to induce slumber, my mind would suddenly come alive with thoughts and questions. We would be up for hours, talking about everything and any-thing, my brain all of a sudden running around with questions about the world and thoughts about life. It was strange, even to me, that these moments would come out of nowhere, when I had spent all day either borderline mute or just running around madly in visions of sporting heroics. It was almost as if we needed to set up an environment where I was totally safe, judgement-free, for me to let go of caution and see where thought and speech took me.

When she wasn't doing that, my dad would sit at the end of my bed and watch late-night American football with me while I tried to do my maths homework. It was quite nice, that time difference, and watching a sport on the other side of the world. He did not know that, in years to come, he would again receive that translucent glow through the night, setting his alarm to watch me play day after day, series after series, of Ashes cricket in Australia. Back then we'd watch until I caught a sight of Dan Marino, the Miami Dolphins quarterback, and then, when Dad realised I wasn't going to take my eyes off the game, he'd finish my homework while I watched Marino make plays. I liked Marino because, being the quarterback, everything ran through him. He was the centre of every single play. The game did not start until he started. He read plays; he sidestepped tackles; he saw things other people didn't see. When he turned up not long after in *Ace Ventura: Pet Detective*, his legendary status in my mind was forever confirmed.

The thing I didn't really envy about Dan Marino was the bodies flying at him constantly, looking like they were trying to decapitate him. It was the only undesirable thing about doing what he did and a suspicion I had confirmed when I was a teenager and was asked to play rugby for the club. They'd seen me play other sports and thought, given I was quite fast, that I would be a useful winger in the last ten minutes. I am a substitute and watch in fear as 16-stone teenagers absolutely mash each other up. My first piece of action is having a Jonah Lomu-type player running at me. He is the size of buildings. I stick my arm out and he runs through me like a turnstile. Later on in the game, I get the ball on the wing and do what I've been told – I ran as fast as I can to the try line. I brace for impact, race off and, incredibly, feel no one get near me to begin with. As I see the line getting closer, hoovering it towards me, flailing chunky arms in my peripheries and hearing a stampede in my wake, I forget to take heed of Burnley's classically unsteady playing grounds. There is a little crater that my foot goes through and, on impact, my legs just buckle completely. I admit defeat and do not clamber back directly to my feet. In the second I'm lying there, waiting for oceans of boys much bigger than me to throw their whole weight on top of me, I unclutch the ball, leaving it easier for them to dispossess me, and promise myself I will never play this stupid game again.

All of these heroes and attributes and sports begin to stack up in my mind. I am collating them as I go, throwing myself into them, trying to fit them and make them fit me. I can play basketball, adding Magic Johnson to the hero collection from 'NBA Jam' on the Game Boy, finding sweet relief in inhabiting his body and inverting my physical lack of height inside the handheld computer game. I can swim. Golf will get me soon. Football really fills up Burnley, the same way it does the rest of the country. One year, my team goes away on a trip to France to play a seven-a-side tournament. I find a way to try and contribute in as many ways as I can, to read the game as intensely as possible, to be as versatile as physically achievable for the team. I am small and not as eye-catching as others, but I make it work for me. In the tournament, a window of play opens where I receive the ball and, cut inside, beat a player, evading their tackle and feel myself suddenly instilled with an outcome that feels pre-destined. From outside the area, I put my laces through the ball and it torpedoes into the top corner. It looks like one of Eric Bristow's darts. I feel myself swell with a sensation of having done something more than I knew I was capable of. As my teammates surround me, chasing after me, I do not make even one single gesture of celebration. I just jog back to my place. I don't think I even smile. When we lost the same tournament on penalties, I felt like I had experienced something as brutal as first heartbreak. These two things – the sensation of occasionally awakening a dormant other-worldliness and the absolute distaste for losing – will never dislodge themselves as unmovable, strange curiosities that are a part of being me.

CHAPTER 10

BURNLEY CC

Cricket is different. There is something about cricket. It is almost as if it takes all of my ideas about sport, these daydreams of who I am going to be, that quiet longing for something else, and holds them all. It says to every aspect of my inner psyche, *We can have you here; we can make sense of it for you.*

My dad is the captain of the Burnley second XI – his father a club cricketer too – and I go to watch them. During the tea break, we drag the bins and plant pots out from by the little pavilion, its purple seats cast-offs from Turf Moor, which overlooks it. They become wickets and extra fielders and we re-enact what we have just seen. At the cricket club, the outside world has a way of muscling into the foreground, lurking and coursing its fingers through everything, as it does in Burnley in general. On the opposite side to the football ground, one-floor houses, some boarded up, look out on to the green, somehow merging with the sight screen, everything the same hue of faded white and grey and blood-red. Set back from them is an old

53

singular cotton mill cutting a shape into the sky. During the off season, to make some money, the pitch is used as a car park for the football, trampled into a sea of flattened grass for fans to use for their convenience, the only remnant being the cordoned-off square for the wicket.

The pitch itself has a ridge in the run-up, making the wicket ripple like a photograph or frozen artefact of the creek that runs over the road not far away, running up and out of the town. There is a slope too. It bears a resemblance to a much more celebrated cricketing slope – the one at the home of cricket – one I have only seen on television and don't dare even dream I will see in real life. But the two, Burnley and Lord's, do blend in the imagination this way, by the quirk of uneven footing, if nothing else.

I spend every day, when I am not at the cricket club or at school, bowling a ball at my garage door. Again and again, I run in and bowl the scuffed and chewed tennis ball. Each time I deliver it, I look back up, losing line of sight of it for a second and catch it hurtling towards the batter-less garage door. *Just do something*, I beg of it. *Spin or swing. Do something magical.*

It does nothing. And yet I still run in, over and over. In the Burnley teams, neither being the biggest nor the most powerful, incredibly slight and wiry by comparison to everyone else, I don't really stand out as a batter or a bowler. I don't know which I am, how I best contribute to anything meaningful. My cousin plays with me and says, give me the strike and I'll hit sixes. I do what he says. I do, though, start to use fielding as a kind of asset. The game seems like it allows for anyone to pop up at any given moment and be a hero, and I search for that myself. I know, from the football tournament, that I am capable of small moments of strange transcendence, occasionally doing something special for no other reason than the constant trying. Once, while playing for the third team, I fly through the air and take a catch, an image of Paul Collingwood in a Test match some years later, plucking the ball while suspended in mid-air, unsure where it came from. For me, every ball is a new beginning, a moment that a catch might sail to my right, or a chance to bowl that delivery I'd been searching for, or for the ball to be so sweetly struck that my gifts as a batter suddenly fall out of the sky and into my lap. Another time, during my innings of 49 not out opening the batting, I search for that for 50 overs. It never comes and I walk back into the dressing room, past the purple stairs to a sea of scowls from teammates for dragging the run rate into disrepute.

I am grateful for Burnley Cricket Club, though, because that's where my friends are. School does not offer the friendships that Burnley CC does. My parents encourage me to be there as much as I want to be, because it makes me happy. I begin to realise, just from spending time at the club, amongst so many different age ranges, that I tend to be a completely different person around different people. My character, the way I behave, the things that fall out of my mouth, can vary wildly depending on the environment I'm in. The length of cricket matches allows me plenty of time to notice things about myself. I realise, for example, how much I observe other people, trying to get a sense and feel for the right way to behave with them and, most importantly, whether I can trust them.

As I start playing in the Burnley third team, I am sharing a dressing room with lots of older people. I am quiet to begin with, just sitting there and watching and listening. But the great thing about being around adults, I find immediately, is that there is not the jostling and bullying, and desperation just to be accepted as part of a pack or a group that can come with teenagers. It simply just feels right. Everyone makes it clear that they have my back and are going to look after me if I need it. That is what this cricket team is about. It gives a swell of something purposeful, a cause to be optimistic about life. It is an unspoken rule that everyone looked after everyone else.

My close mates Gaz Halley and Dave Brown are both a year younger than me, and better cricketers. I meet them at 13 and, as would become a running theme with most of the closest people in my life, we don't initially really get on. They watch me running around after the ball and laugh at my sulking, kicking my cap back to fine leg when I'd bowled badly, but, for whatever reason, they take a shine to me. Out of the three of us, Gaz is the most confident. He helps Dave and me out of any social tangle, but neither of them had friends either at their school and, somewhere in our sub-conscious, we recognise that and form an unspoken, protective circle around each other. They are my interpersonal skills bodyguards, propping me up when I need it in any given social situation.

Anna and Nicole Mortimer are twins who come down to the club because their dad, Neil, plays for the club. The Mortimers' house is a safe place for us all to go and listen to records, to talk about cricket, to hang around. None of them go to my school, and I find a way to reinvent myself in the company of these people. I trust them and they have the confidence and social sparkle that I am struggling to find in myself. We are always at their place. I walk over to the Mortimers' in the early hours to watch the 1992 Cricket World Cup final between England and

Pakistan. I am struck by the pain of England being bundled out in a hurry, but my eye is caught by the bowling of the Pakistani bowler Wasim Akram and the wild movement in the air his deliveries are able to conjure.

All the drinking and the partying and the growing up happens under the same gentle, watchful community support. I smoke two cigarettes and have two pints at the pub, throw up everywhere and have to phone my dad to pick me up from the same place he'd dropped me off an hour earlier. On another occasion, I drink too much and end up in Neil Mortimer's bed when he is out, vomiting in the sheets. I pull them over, don't say a word to anyone, and pretend it didn't happen. Neil is so nice that he doesn't even mention it. I'm sure my parents would have arranged to get those cleaned. I don't ask. Just don't mention it, pretend it hasn't happened, hope it goes away.

We spend our time at Neil's rifling through his record collection, going through CDs and drinking the beers he'd left out for us – always enough to be grateful, to feel like adults, never enough to actually get drunk.

Gaz and I dye our hair for the first time during these years, peroxiding it together in his mum's bathroom. We use plastic bags, making a hole in it and pulling hair through in handfuls to bleach individual clumps. Gaz holds his nerve longer than me, making sure it is left in for long enough. I can feel it burning, singeing its way into my scalp. Panicking and tip-toeing back and forth in the tiny bathroom, I rinse it off. My hair ends up the exact colour and, more strangely, the texture of Big Bird on *Sesame Street*. It doesn't go down well at school, and the next time I see Gaz, I discover that he too had been sent back home and had shaved it all off.

Slightly less painful hair dyeing then ensues at the Mortimers', who also allow us our first trip to see the band James in Manchester. We take the X43 bus, wide-eyed and collectively bracing for a non-Burnley world. I only realise on arrival that I've lost the tickets. We don't have a lot of money, any of us, and spend an hour in a panic outside the MEN Arena in our Marks & Spencers hand-me-down clothes, worrying that our night is over before it has begun. A tout takes pity on us and hands back some tickets on the cheap. We have the night of our lives, singing James songs all the way home.

The first time I go to Old Trafford Cricket Ground is a semi-final one-day game against Yorkshire. The team is full of international cricketers – of superhero-like players, so close you can almost touch them. Wasim Akram, Mike Atherton, Jason Gallian, John Crawley, Neil Fairbrother, Graham Lloyd, Mike Watkinson, Gary Yates, Warren Hegg, Glen Chapple, Peter Martin, Ian Austin. Seeing them in person makes them real – them playing under a darkened Mancunian sky making them seem at once mercurial and everyday. I travel to see them in the final at Lord's too, with my dad and my mum's brother, Mark. It's the first time I've seen Lord's, bending my head to make sense of the slope, awed at the magnitude of it all. Lancashire win, despite an Aravinda de Silva hundred, and I watch everyone who has made the same car trips down with their families run across the ground, filling the regal space with joy as the Lancs players wave from the dressing room, drinks aloft.

Gaz and I get jobs at Burnley Football Club in the summer of 2000, the year they sign Ian Wright. We work at the ticket office and they send Ian around. It is the first time I have met an actual sporting hero and I shake his hand for slightly too long as he does the rounds with the staff. It is quite a special experience, but not special enough to install sufficient respect for Gaz and I to think twice about playing headers and volleys on the pitch at half-time in front of the cricket field stand. We are very quickly escorted off by the general manager, Andrew Watson, and told our time with the football club has come to an end.

As our clothes get trendier (I find myself becoming particularly besotted with the play on words French Connection has conjured up with FCUK IT), the three of us bundle into many unsuccessful, awkward and left-field dating escapades. I regularly find myself feeling incredibly out of my depth on these, and often come up with quite ill-thought-out ways to bail. I leave a message on a pizza box for one girl when she left for a minute, writing that I'd had a 'family emergency', and 'apologies for the impromptu departure' on top of it. Another time, I leave via the back door of the Manor Barn pub when I realise that we are on dates with women over twice our age.

We spend that off season playing pool at Rileys, Gaz skipping work so that he can meet me for sausage and chips. We do strange, sporty things for teenagers to do, like play squash. We stay at a girl's house while telling our parents that we are staying at each other's. It's a weeks-long, pre-arranged, meticulously planned ruse, only for me to accidentally order a takeaway back to my own house and blow the whole thing open. I split my head open on a drainpipe outside Gaz's house, pretending to head-butt it and kicking it with my foot to make the sound, only to actually head-butt it. His mum has to look after me, dressing my wound and explaining that my slapstick needs a bit of work. It is all very regular teenage escapades, no one with much of an idea what we are doing or what our futures hold, just bundling ourselves from one moment to the next, only stopping to watch *Red Dwarf* or Lee Evans or Victoria Wood.

I balance this sort of new *joie de vivre* in some of these everyday 'teenager meets world' outings with a real ability to sulk on a cricket pitch when things aren't going my way. After all, I am still nowhere near the bowler or cricketer I want to be. It isn't offering me any realistic way out. I can't even get out of the thirds. When I bowl badly, I have, what the Burnley players call then, an 'absolute cob on' for hours. I just can't hide it. It becomes me. It feels like the world is closing in on me. All I want is for sport to go right, for the ball to bend to my will.

At Smackwater Jacks at the weekends, everyone from Burnley who is out is out there. It's divided into two floors and there is an unwritten rule for everyone. All the school kids and teenagers are on the first floor, and all the adults are on the ground floor. We are kicking our feet around on the first floor, fumbling our way around conversations, and Gaz says, 'Shall we see what the adults are doing?' They are all at least 15 years older than us, and yet, because they know us from the cricket club, they treat us like we are just with them. It's an access I wouldn't have without cricket and, on the ground floor of Smacks, I feel much more at home. There is no tension or hyper fixation on weaknesses or herd mentality, I just feel allowed to be myself here, whoever that is. Upstairs is full of people who think they're the big time, and I can't bear it. Cricket is not like that, I think to myself on this floor.

It somehow carves people out, shapes them into an acceptance of themselves, settles them in their skin. Next stop, Panama Joe's. It's ten pence a pint there.

It was all so normal. We were all doing the same thing. Nothing in those summers, in all that messing around, all that longing, all that trying and failing, gave anyone the sense of what was to come knocking.

CHAPTER 11

GROWTH SPURT

We had all done exactly the same stuff in the off season as we always did. It was a winter away from cricket, a time to run around and play other sports. There was no working on my snap or wrist position or secret tutoring. There was nothing remarkable or different about anything I had done compared to any of the other winters. I'm expecting to come back the same player – trying hard, regularly kicking my jumper or cap away in disgust, harbouring a longing to be someone else – with Gaz and Dave, let alone everyone else, much better than me.

We are back in the nets and Dave's dad, the first team captain, is facing up. He's getting some time batting himself in against the kids, but as I run in, I suddenly sense myself to be ten times stronger than the last time I bowled. It's exhilarating, like I've been topped up in some sort of computer game, extra lives fizzing me towards the crease. I let go and the process is like lightning, the approach, the coil, the delivery, the speed the ball leaves my hand. Dave's dad, visibly stretched and taken by surprise, puts his bat down to block the ball, slightly squared up. The ball hits it and, in a moment of life-changing drama and destruction, a teenage year's worth of dreaming manifested, the Kookaburra Bubble shatters into six or seven different shards of wood. He is just standing there, looking at me with a puzzled expression on his face, still grasping the bat's handle, which is now the only part of it remaining. I am shocked too and receive his look before glancing back at my right hand that has delivered the ball. It looks the same, but as I stare quizzically into my open palm, it is as if it is twitching. I feel like Peter Parker, suddenly handed something superhuman.

I have not just gathered a yard of pace, I'm maybe 15 or 20 miles an hour quicker. I'm bowling genuinely fast. To suddenly be able to do this thing gives me a sheer rush of adrenaline and power. *What happens if I bowl short?* I ask myself. I might be able to even rush these guys, scare them a bit. I run in the same way towards the next senior player and, doing my best impression of what I imagine scary fast bowlers do, muscle the ball into the middle of the pitch as if it is a trampoline. It veers short of a length and hits the next batter on the head. He walks away rattled. I apologise and turn around, confused and giddy. With great power comes great responsibility, I do not think to myself then but should have.

I come back the next day praying that I hadn't imagined this, or that the speed and the way the ball has suddenly been blessed with a new energy isn't a strange anomaly, a one-night-only experience. But it is still there. It is part of my muscle memory now, the feel, the rhythm and the speed. They are not all wicket-taking balls – there are many wides, balls that fly off the pitch one side and then the other the following ball. I bowl more than four wides an over, frantically running in as I try to control this newfound speed. But in amongst it, I am managing to find balls that visibly shock players.

Martin van Jaarsveld is a travelling pro. He faces me first ball of a game, and as I am at my mark, my captain at mid-off says, 'Bounce him first ball; he won't be expecting it to be as quick as it will be.' I nod, take a deep breath and do what he says. When the ball leaves my hand, I lose sight of it for a second, before looking back up to see his body language implode while the ball is in flight, as if he is a boxer who had his gloves by his side prepared for a mismatch and then suddenly is trying to raise them in fright. He gloves it straight to the captain. I get other pros out too, including Roger Harper who nicks off a more classical delivery. Then Australian Brad Hodge, a serious scalp, fending a wayward beamer off his face with his gloves, who turns to me to say, 'Fuck off, you little prick,' before I bowl him. It is the kind of relationship with Australians that I will one day cultivate for fun. It is in these moments where I start to feel that if I can do this to these guys, maybe I can do it to anyone.

John Stanworth, the academy director, calls me up and gets me into play for Lancashire under-17s. I don't mention that I have been for trials before, at 12 and 14, and got nowhere near. I feel like someone else now. Kyle Hogg and Saj Mahmood are both a similar age to me and, rounded up from our different universes, all three of us can bowl much quicker than anyone else. As we progress into the Lancashire team, each one of us fuelling the other, there is no time to really think about the circumstances taking me there alongside them, it's all just forward momentum, running in fast, thoughtless and effortless.

CHAPTER 12

LANCASHIRE

2002

It's my first delivery ever as a professional cricketer, for Lancashire's second XI. We are playing Surrey's second team at Stanley Park, Blackpool. I run in and, as I do, my legs become unstable. Halfway through the stride, I become unfamiliar with what bowling even is; nerves have rendered me an empty shell. As I get to the crease, it feels as though I'm attempting an impression of a bowler. I jump at the crease. I've never tried to jump at the crease before. I am, somehow, as if trying to rewind time, jumping backwards, ball still in hand. As I land, my back foot takes out both the leg and middle stump and I fall in a heap. Before I even dare look up, the umpire, Ian Gould, is talking to me. 'What the hell was that, son?' he asks.

This is the cost of the sequence of events since the breaking of the bat in Burnley; things have happened really quickly, mostly good and sometimes bad. It's like driving a fast car I have no control of. I've been starting to consistently scare older men, county pros, bowling quickly without really thinking about it. It's like all the years of wishing and trying have stored up and exploded inside me. I've been handed a trial and, despite falling into the stumps occasionally and going through periods of bowling with a radar that is set to spin, I have been successful and landed in a Lancashire squad with a whole host of street-smart, wise, older international cricketers: Peter Martin, Neil Fairbrother, Glen Chapple, Mike Watkinson, Warren Hegg, Mike Atherton and Ian Austin. They are all Lancastrian and have a kind of inbuilt community spirit in bringing through other Lancastrian cricketers. I am one. The ball is going everywhere when I bowl it, sometimes bowling people, turning them inside out, sometimes rushing them for pace, sometimes going very far down the leg side. Occasionally, it moves in the air, but I don't really know exactly how I am doing that, it just sometimes does.

Mike Watkinson is playing for the first team and coaching the second team. I know Mike from afar, a Test cricketer who had adapted his game from a medium pace bowler to an off spinner and eventually earned England caps doing the latter at the back end of his career. He learned it as a league cricketer, running in as fast as he could until his body had not allowed him, reverting to off spin and then finding his way. The first time he'd seen himself bowl was the Benson and Hedges Cup final in 1984. He had played as a professional cricketer his whole life and never once seen himself bowl. He looked at himself on the television replay and wondered why he had a 20-metre run-up that he was doing at a right angle. Nobody had told him to do anything else. Mike learned so much about watching footage of himself just once that he had set up a camera to film the younger bowlers too. When I see footage of myself back for the first time, I am horrified. I don't see the good stuff – I have really good rotation, a rhythmical action and a natural illusion that creates the impression the ball is going too straight, always diving in at a batter, asking them to play at everything. I just think it looks horrible.

Mike is like a cricketing sensei. He watches me squirm a little bit, just at seeing my own reflection, and then asks a few uncomplicated questions. Some balls were going wayward and some were perfect, he said. We are playing a second team game at Middleton Cricket Club and in the first innings I've bowled more of the wayward than the wonderful, stropping my way back to fine leg and my mark like the world has caved in every time I do so. He only says a few words after the questions. He talks about the relationship between the index finger and the second finger. The pad of the second finger, he says, is where you want to be feeling the ball for the longest for the outswinger. Maybe try pointing that seam towards second slip, he says, too. The last thing that is in control of that ball is the tip of the finger, he tells me. That's where all the control is, just the feeling of it leaving the hand there. I do not know it yet but this is where, many years later, the deep calluses will have built up, after having felt that feeling so much, and learned to rely on it as my only real tell about how I am bowling. There's a brief discussion about the flick of the fingers. The ball, he tells me, will start rotating backwards on its axis. His speech is concise and direct, as if he is gifting me the natural laws of the universe, and suddenly it all makes sense.

We briefly discuss the inswinger too, talking about the same technique but the feeling coming from the index finger instead, the ball pointing at leg slip. If you can master both of these, he says, you will be able to do something not many people have ever done.

I have the ball on a string during the second innings. There is no guessing, no running on the back of a strange energy like I've mounted a manic horse, but actual control. It goes exactly where I want it every time. It was true, it was all *feel*. Later that year, Mike will select me to open the bowling with Kyle Hogg in the first team. I was 17 and he was 19. My first wicket is Ian Ward, caught behind by Warren Hegg. I had landed in the perfect storm that season, where all my willing and wildness was met with a group of cricketers who knew exactly where to point it. Warren Hegg, captain and wicketkeeper of that team, would have periods when he told me not to worry at all about the field or anything, just bowl as fast as I could. Then Mike would be softly preaching the arts when I needed it, with other great seamers like Glen Chapple and Peter Martin always watching and helping. If it hadn't been for them that year, I would have been happy just to run myself into a puppyish frenzy for a few years, taking wickets, bowling wides and going back to Burnley satisfied with a ragtag career in the County game.

The lifestyle at Lancashire and welcoming into County Cricket is like an awakening into an adult world, disarmingly everyday for one that requires actual athleticism. Gary Keedy is my roommate and, every morning without fail, the moment he wakes up, before he even opens his eyes, he fumbles around for a cigarette. I'm in the bed next door to him and become accustomed to my alarm being the smell of smoke. He wouldn't even turn the light on, I would just wake to the orange glow of his first cigarette. Half of the team smoke and during practice or games, the first team congregate on the second team balcony to light up. Benson and Hedges are sponsoring the one-day tournament too and, with every round you progress, someone will turn up with a pack of duty-free, comedy-sized boxes of cigarettes. All the smokers get free rein, passing them around themselves. It still felt so recently that I'd tried to smoke at 15 and thrown up and had to be picked up by my dad. That and Gary Keedy's smoke alarm was enough to put me off the whole thing.

I am still living at home, bouncing back and forth from this new abnormal and what I have always known. To get to practice, my mum and dad drive me to the McDonald's 20 minutes outside of Burnley, in Haslingden. Stranded between stations, I wait, struck by how much McDonald's and cigarettes there are in a professional cricketer's life, before Graham Lloyd picks me up. When Graham can't, Joe Scuderi does. He gets me to meet him at his house, where he has a shrine to Kiss, and we listen to AC/DC and hair metal all the way into Old Trafford.

For some reason, I start to go to Glam and Go Tanning Salon in Burnley, turning back up to Lancashire County games bronzed and with bleached highlights in my hair. *I'm going to have to bowl well now*, I think to myself. You can't go to Glam and Go, be singing guitar riffs you've just learnt under your breath, turn up at Lancashire all bronzed when everyone knows you haven't been on holiday and then serve up wides. Ever since Mark Harvey had driven back to Burnley, his Lancashire deal just signed and a Peugeot 206 with his name on the side, that's all I'd wanted. I got mine too.

CHAPTER 13

ONE DAY DEBUT

15 December 2002

AUSTRALIA vs ENGLAND, 2nd ODI, *Melbourne*

Australia 318/6; England 229

Australia won by 89 runs

Australia innings: **A Gilchrist b Anderson 124; J Anderson 6–0–46–1**

Inside the belly of the MCG, it feels like it is all darkness. I've been told only a few days ago by Nigel Lawton from the Academy in Adelaide that England want me to travel to join the squad. They are mid-Ashes series, having a torrid time and lots of bowlers have been sent home, injured. Nasser Hussain has only told me yesterday, to my deep surprise, that I am playing. In one sentence, spat out of his mouth, less as an honour and more as if he was recruiting to the Army, I go from a tourist to an England international.

I've waited as long as I can so as not to wake up my parents, but finally buckled at 5am, phoning home, to tell them I am going to be playing for England today. It's been only five years since the days of bunking off school to walk to the outskirts of Burnley. My parents are living in the same house as back then. I don't mention to them that I have already got the kit out of the bag and I'm wearing it in my own hotel room. I'm just looking at myself in the mirror, Vodafone emblazoned on the front of my shirt, double-checking again and again that it is real. It's like trying on an alter-ego Superman costume for the first time. It says it's medium, but it hangs off me, incredibly loose and ill-fitting. As I look at myself, I keep seeing flashes of Tom Hanks in *Big*, a child finding himself suddenly drenched in oversized men's clothes, a wish granted. I find it hard to recognise myself. It feels good.

There's no sign of a cricket pitch as we enter the stadium, it's like being in the bowels of an alien aircraft, the stamping of a crowd you still cannot see cannoning off the underground car park. As we walk out of the dressing room, back through the car park and up a ramp, the spikes on my shoes echo with a sense of fragility. Just out of sight, up the hill, there's a bright, blinding light. As we get closer, I feel my stride lengthening, walking myself higher and further, beyond the car park towards the pitch. For a split second, it is difficult to distinguish the distance and time between those Burnley truant walks and the walk here now. It is almost as if by simply wishing to be someone else I have become this person now. Who that is, I am not yet sure. And neither is anyone else. Due to the lateness of my emergency call-up, the huge ballooning shirt has no name on the back. I am not just unknown to myself, but literally unknown to anyone. The Melbourne Cricket Ground, like those escape routes in Burnley, also tests you, dares you to walk up that ramp and into that coliseum. For some, the game is already lost just on that walk.

Everyone else in the team wears shirts with their name on, most of them players I only know from television; people I was idolising years ago, film stars I hadn't even imagined to be real. Even these hardened professionals look a bit overawed, walking out at the MCG next to me, looking as if they are circling 360 degrees on the way to the middle, just trying to somehow process the largeness of the ground and the odd inverted vertigo that comes from being in the middle of it. It is a huge, stacked, concrete block of seats, with no eyeline or horizon beyond it. It is a cricket stadium so removed from the one in Burnley I have spent my life playing on that it hardly resembles the same sport. I am opening the bowling and fielding at fine leg, right next to Bay 13. No one has told me that fielding in front of Bay 13 is a kind of initiation reserved for new players, somewhere no one else wants to go, famed as it is for being the rowdiest part of the stadium. I am standing there, no name, my back to the baying masses, trying to ignore the insults. They are shouting 'who are you?' and 'water boy', again and again. They are constantly reminding me of my blank shirt, that no one has seen or heard of me before, that I am just making up the numbers, that they are never going to see me again. They are enlarged, mammoth versions of my own internal voice on that hilltop Burnley bench only five years ago, devilishly transformed into thousands of Australian accents.

This is the story that I know from the outside too. The Australians are the winners; the gloating, relentless, goading, frothing at the mouth for more winners. It is baked into who they are, never stopping for a second to consider the foot coming off the throat. England finishing second best to Australia is all I know. I understand the heartbreak and the longing and the self-punishment that comes from being an English cricket supporter completely. Now that I am inside, it plays out in a flash of verification, that the power dynamic is exactly how I imagined. They mould in my imagination to the boys from school too – surrounded by laughter, wondering who I am, as I wait, shrunk and small, an experience of nothing else but being less than.

The game is already looking ominously done by the time I am bowling to Adam Gilchrist in the 38th over. He has 124 and Australia are 240/1. I have, like everyone else, been spending my teens watching him, awestruck, as he put England teams to the sword. I run in. It's not a great ball, outside off stump. Gilchrist swings as freely as he has been all afternoon, as freely as he has been all decade, but this time he mistimes it and inside edges the ball on to his own stumps. In slight shock, I run towards the stumps, as if to check that is what has happened. The commentary team, unbeknownst to me, has called me Jimmy Adams as I do so. I've done it, I've taken a wicket, but still nobody knows my name.

By the time I have to bat, they can only find me a fielding helmet to wear. It's an extension of the cumbersome, strange-fit kit that my first game comes with. It has an extra bar across the front, just to really help impair my vision. I am squinting into the concrete blocks, trying to find any way of getting close to the rockets Brett Lee is throwing with a scuffed-up white ball under lights. I don't even see the one he bowls me with, just hear the clatter of the stumps and walk off, back into the cavernous abyss of the car park. It was like that walk back from school, shrugging and hoping that I'd be back.

CHAPTER 14

OH JIMMY, JIMMY

22 February 2003

**ENGLAND vs PAKISTAN, 2003 Cricket World Cup,
Cape Town**

England 246/8; Pakistan 134 all out
England won by 112 runs
Pakistan innings: **J Anderson 10–2–29–4**

The England team travel straight from Australia to South Africa
for the World Cup. I'm selected and have travelled straight there
with them. It feels like I've just been scooped up, caught in the
momentum of a chaotic dream. In the England team, things
are organised for you. Hotels are nicer, no one is sharing.
You are bundled into buses and planes and cricket grounds and
hotels and meeting rooms; all wearing the same thing. As we
travel, I find myself suddenly with better-fitting kit, a number –
40 – and my name on the shirt too. It's tempting to never take

it off when I get back to the hotel room. Just to process, this is real, this is actually happening to me. It is so many things at once – like living out a fantasy and a sort of nervous nightmare too. I am in the team for the World Cup, scratching my head and looking through the names and wondering if that means I am actually in England's best XI, mumbling my way through the days, silently sitting there, watching and rubbing my eyes at all these players who were heroes to me until so recently, being in my space, my teammates.

Cape Town is beautiful, but on the drive from the airport to the cricket ground, there are lots of townships. It's like travelling through different worlds, in a very short space of time. I'm beginning to grow accustomed to that. The ground there is one of the most stunning in the world – the stands are beautifully done, artfully and tastefully with an old grass bank to sit on, with the backdrop of Table Mountain framing it.

We bat first and Shoaib Akhtar is bowling. Shoaib is famous for being possibly the fastest bowler of all time. I sat and watched him on television in the 1999 World Cup in England, running in like some sort of velociraptor hunting out prey; smart and methodical and unflinchingly destructive. Seeing him in the flesh, in real life, really is like seeing some sort of extinct beast, brought back to life in a different universe by a quirk of genetic engineering. He really is that other-worldly. When we bat, he bowls a ball that hits 100 miles an hour on the speed gun. Nick Knight just calmly tucks it off his hip for one, as if it was nothing. This is a different universe. Everything is heightened. Everything is unflinching.

This time, I'm not batting in a fielder's helmet and its extra bar either, although when I see what Akhtar has just bowled,

I wish I was. We score 246/8 in our 50 overs and I am spared needing to bat.

It's the first time my dad and grandad have ever seen me play for England. They've flown out, breathing it in, rubbing their eyes too. I am opening the bowling and, two overs in, Inzamam-ul-Haq arrives at the crease. Inzi is similar in presence and stature to Shoaib Akhtar. As he sets up to face his first ball, his stance, the way he is hunched over his bat, both idiosyncratically elegant and cumbersome, is so familiar to me that it appears he has been green-screened on to the pitch, like I'm in some kind of futuristic simulator. It's *the* Inzamam-ul-Haq. I run in, enthused by the vision of Shoaib I have just seen. I'm not even trying to bowl fast or run fast, I just do. Something else is in my system, willing me on, carrying me towards the wicket, ushering that ball out of my hand. I know it's a good one immediately. Bowling is like that; as soon as it's left your hand, you often just know. Inzi thinks the ball is going straight and opens his body to try and hit it through midwicket, on the leg side. I know it's going to shape, I've felt it tell me that as it's left my hand. As it does, swinging aggressively and suddenly from a middle stump line away from him, his famous outline is frozen, almost painting an S-shape in the air, realising the ball is not going where he expected and trying to adjust. It's too late. It's hit the outside edge and flies to Nick Knight, who catches the ball at his throat, mouth wide open as if he can't believe what's happened either.

As Mohammad Yousuf walks in, another cricketer as heralded and majestic as the others, a self-belief washes through my system. Inzamam looked exactly like those club cricketers playing Burnley that year. I'd bowled the same ball at them too and seen them respond exactly the same way. My best ball was good enough for the best. I don't think I'd ever had proof of it before. Now I do, there is a transformation that takes place in me, a rush of endorphins which somehow switches some vital part of my DNA, telling me I might just belong. As I run in with the next ball, I remember the team meeting the night before. The plan for Yousuf is full and straight, first up. I can do that. I reach for the magic ball, program it into my system, tell the ball what I want it to do. Again, I know, even before it leaves my hand, that it is going to be a good one. It's perfect – a spearing yorker that appears again to be heading down the leg side, then, like a homing missile, 90 miles an hour, straightens at the last minute, leaving Yousuf to force his bat down at the wrong angle while stuck on the crease. I don't see, his body obstructing the angle, taut and guessing still, but I hear the stumps hit. I'm running towards him, helicoptering my arms, screaming and screaming, running into the arms of cricketers I had not even imagined to be real people until recently – Alec Stewart, Marcus Trescothick, Craig White – looking back at them as they ruffle my hair and laugh in my face. If I could have told the boy on that bench in Burnley, with that ham sandwich, I would. But I was something different now, a trajectory taking me elsewhere. It doesn't strike me then, but it will one day, that the boy on the bench is called James. James is the one there still longing, still feeling quite sensitive about everything, worried about social interactions, working out the world. The name they are singing in the crowds now, that's someone else. 'Jimmy' is the person with the ball in his hand.

And in this new skin, it occurs to me as we leave the pitch how much the goalposts have just changed in my life, because as my dad congratulated me against the backdrop of a huge statement of a win against global giants, all I can think about is getting the last ball of my spell wrong, it going for four and Nasser shouting, from behind me at mid-on 'Fuuuuck'.

There was a new territory that came with this world, with this success, and it was the shifting sand of nothing, ever, being enough.

CHAPTER 15

THE AUSSIES

2 March 2003

ENGLAND vs AUSTRALIA, 2003 Cricket World Cup, Gqeberha

England 204/8; Australia 208/8

Australia won by 2 wickets

Australia innings: **J Anderson 9−0−66−0**

The downside of sudden expectation, of quickly becoming known and being part of an opponent's preparations, landed during that same World Cup. The surprise on those Pakistani legends' faces, looking back as I ran towards them celebrating, trying to work out who I was, was gone from then on in. It didn't matter what level of cricket I was playing now; from Burnley to Brisbane, I wasn't going to be running in again with that outsider's sense of abandon. And by the time we met Australia at Port Elizabeth, we had become handicapped and in desperate need of a win because we refused to play in Zimbabwe during Mugabe's reign. A letter had come to the ECB promising to send us 'back to Britain in wooden coffins'. So, it felt like a good idea not to go really, however badly we wanted to finally win a World Cup.

Honestly, I had my suspicions about how far we were going to go in the World Cup anyway when sitting in the dressing room, with Alec Stewart talking to Ian Blackwell. 'I think we have got a really good chance in this tournament,' Alec is saying. 'And it's my last tournament, I really want to win it.' Blackwell nods. 'So, make sure that you eat and drink well and stay healthy because it really could be the difference.' Blackwell nods again and, as if reassuring Stewart, putting his mind to rest, says, 'Don't worry, mate, I'm not drinking beer this tour, just spirits.' It was like I saw the light in Alec Stewart's eyes go out even from across the room.

Whereas Pakistan and other countries had come with a sort of glaze of stardom to them when I first met them, it was different with Australia. Through the television screens and every single cricket conversation I'd ever heard, it had been baked into me from a young age that England lost to Australia. I knew the pain, the heartbreak, the outrage, the searching, the praying from the outside. So, when I am inside, I feel less star-struck about it and more a responsibility on behalf of every English cricket fan I've ever known, to not be part of the same story, to somehow rewrite this pre-written script we were all resigned to. I thought maybe it was coming easily too when, despite bowling a bit out of sorts and at an expensive rate, we had them 135/8 chasing our total of 204.

It's strange how quickly it happened, between Michael Bevan and Andy Bichel. How the story of the game reversed, a sort of inevitability kicking in and just dragging the result to the same one we had always known. How it felt like we were just part of a loss that had already been played out before and we were bound to play out forever. I felt it, like heaviness in my feet, as they clawed the runs back and eventually only required 14 from the last two overs. I couldn't believe it when Nasser threw me the ball, and not Andrew Caddick, for the penultimate over. I almost felt like telling him he'd made a mistake, that surely he didn't want me to bowl this over that would decide the game. In my peripheries I could see Caddick, hands on hips, thinking the same thing. I could almost hear him muttering.

The ball did not do what I wanted. None of the effortlessness fell out of my bones. Instead, Andy Bichel, a bowler by trade, picks up my second ball and despatches me for six over midwicket, before carting me down the ground on the leg side for another four. The game was done. I had blown it. I left the field in what felt like dusk, dust everywhere, now part of a story I'd seen from the outside, an English defeat against Australia, somehow snatching defeat from the jaws of victory.

Nasser put his arm around me in the dressing room straight after, my head bowed, putting away my gear, and simply said, 'I could have given Caddick that over. I wanted you to bowl it.' He was telling me that he trusted me and that he would do it again. It was supposed to help me, and in a way it did, but I just felt the cloud, that darkness of losing, the same as it had felt in the garden against my dad all those years ago; no bigger and no smaller. What Nasser didn't tell me is that months later, when I get him out as the second of a hat-trick against Essex, hitting him on the boot, he goes back to the dressing room and tells his teammates, in a rage, 'He never does that when I ask him.'

CHAPTER 16

TEST DEBUT

22 May 2003

ENGLAND vs ZIMBABWE, 1st Test, Lord's

England 472; Zimbabwe 147 & 233 (following on)

England won by an innings and 92 runs

Zimbabwe first innings: **J Anderson 16–4–73–5**

Here I am, suddenly sitting in the England dressing room at Lord's, where I watched all those Lancashire fans run across the pitch. Then I was on the outside, now I am on the inside and selected to play in a Test match. Even though I have taken the first ever hat-trick in a one day game for England just a month before, it is all so surreal. I have walked the stairs, poked my head around the long room, ran my hands up the staircase, stared at the portraits of greats gone by, reached out and touched the surfaces as if to test if it is all as expensive as it looks, then waited until all the regulars have got in. It is still surreal in itself to attach actual human beings to the names I have been watching from television as a Burnley club cricketer only a year ago: Trescothick, Vaughan, Butcher, Hussain, Key, Stewart. The list goes on.

I am on debut with Anthony McGrath from Yorkshire, much older than me, his body language much more suited to this kind of thing. He looks like he has had a lifetime more than me to ready himself and yet both of us wait to find our spot, making sure we are not in anyone's territory. Eventually, I am just sitting in a corner, as still as I can be, trying to blend into the surroundings. It's not the easiest thing to do given my hair is bleached blond, and I can tell that my hair, contrasting against my near-mute approach to socialising, plus the way I bowl, is making me a hard figure to read for all the stalwarts in the dressing room. I'm finding myself hard to read. I am a collection of fizzing nerves, all this psychedelic information on the life of a Test cricketer unfolding in front of me. I just sit there, trying to watch, pick up who sits where and how the rhythm of it all works. I have been in the company of the one-day side on tour, but there's something about the *whites*, about this being *Test cricket*, that this is very definitely, actually *Lord's*, which is giving it all a surreal glow.

Darren Gough opens his cricket bag – a huge coffin full of gear, new and old – and over his shoulder I see he has a list of leading Test wicket-takers marked inside it, written down in permanent marker. Some names are crossed off. I realise, without wanting to give away that I'm looking too hard, that he is ticking off the bowlers he has gone past in world cricket. *I have no Test wickets*, I think to myself, the inside of his bag appearing like Mount Rushmore as I squint to read who is on there. It is obvious there is a rivalry between him and his fast bowling partner, Andy Caddick. They do not sit together. Nothing is said; there is just an energy there where you can feel that inside this room are all kinds of different loaded, personal and pressurised competitions.

As we get ready for the first morning's play, there is not a coldness per se, but a tension that I haven't experienced in a dressing room before. I look around it, scanning it for safe places, maybe next to Ashley Giles? Perhaps Steve Harmison or Matthew Hoggard? I come to realise there is no one remotely my age. This is not the kind of age difference as reassurance that I had been tractor-beamed towards at Smackwater Jack's ground floor, or the sort of coming of age, lessons of life way I experienced in the Lancashire packs, who prioritised bringing in younger players. Here, there is a wariness; a sense that there is something precious to be lost here, that there is sacred ground that must be protected. Nasser Hussain and Duncan Fletcher have been hauling the England side into a new era for four years. Their considerable, if still gradual, upward curve is not to do with freedom of expression or the joys of being a group. It is about not losing. It is about having the stomach to fight and resist and after English cricket has been criticised heavily for so long, all the players in there, heroes to me, look slightly worn, wary, jaded, all talking themselves silently into going back out to fight another round. The inconsistency in selection for the many preceding years has left everyone protective and paranoid, and with it there is a feeling of players hoping to do enough to keep their place, above and beyond thinking what it might take to win a game of Test cricket.

Duncan Fletcher – from where I am now – is quite intimidating.

He is steely-faced, looking like he is often deep inside his own thoughts. We do not communicate much. I just listen, always listen. Over the years, he will help me with my batting, and I will develop a respect for him and the way he has wrestled English cricket back from the brink. Him and Nasser are resuscitating the game, and when you are doing that, you don't always have time to look around and make sure if everyone's comfortable. That works for me. I have no urge to do anything but blend in, observe, learn and, more than anything else, bowl.

I've been on the pitch twice before I get to run in my most natural habitat; on the pitch with Anthony McGrath to receive our caps, and then to bat. I am using someone else's bat. It has no stickers or sponsors on it. Quite early on against Heath Streak, I feel the ball hit my pad and then cannon straight onto the middle of my bat for four. It's definitely out and definitely hit my pad first, but no one appeals. As always, I stay still, saying nothing, I just blink and gulp and hope for good luck.

As Zimbabwe begin their first innings, I have never stood at my mark and been so nervous. Matthew Hoggard has bowled the first over from the Pavilion End and I've just waited in the field as he does, watching his oddly familiar hustle, feeling strangely too close to it, knowing I will be next. I receive the ball, mark my run-up and for a momentary second reconsider if I even know how long my run-up is. Only two or three years ago I had been second best to Gaz Halley and Dave Brown while playing in Burnley's third team, kicking that jumper around. It was only a year ago that I fell over in front of the stumps for Lancashire seconds. It's only a handful of years since the journeys to that bench. Some coming-of-age films flicker through my mind: Macaulay Culkin asking whether he made his family disappear or Tom Hanks again in *Big*. I feel my tongue clamped down at the side of my mouth between my teeth, the giveaway I'm uncomfortable, that something is alien to me.

Nasser Hussain, our relationship until now a series of clipped sentences where he either praises or apologises to me, or screams obscenities in my general direction and I say nothing, comes up to me. 'Don't worry about the field,' he says. 'Just focus on the bowling.' There is no fine leg. It's the first time I've bowled to a field with no fine leg. Do I say anything? No, I say nothing. He must know best; he's the England captain, I think. It's like the broken wrist on that black ice or the sick in Neil Mortimer's bed. I know something is up, but I choose to say nothing. Better just to keep schtum and try to do what I'm told. The over is a disaster. Seventeen runs are leaked off my first ever six balls in Test cricket, most of them down to the eerily vacated spot at fine leg. I can't remember if I've ever conceded 17 runs in an over in my life.

As is becoming our general mode of communication, Nasser walks over to me for the next one. I'm half expecting him to take the ball out of my hands, send me to the boundary to deal with a fate far worse than Bay 13, my own shame, but he says instead, 'I got that wrong,' looking at the ball and not at me. 'Don't worry about that one.' He resets the field, this time much more something I am accustomed to seeing. I settle, breathe out, set off and start again. Cricket always gives you a chance to reset and start again. By the third over, I'm beginning to mould into the hum of Lord's a little, finding it less stressful, my line and length corrected, blending into the sweet spell of doing what I can do. Mark Vermeulen is facing me. I run in, calmer, through my usual process, the grass beneath me more accommodating than it had been even five minutes ago, a wind behind me, feeling the slope, the gentle uphill that ties Lord's to Burnley and the creek. I'm into my stride, briefly sighting my watch on my left wrist that will one day be replaced by a wristband. I follow the line of it and the ball does too. Vermeulen has guessed the wrong line and plays inside of it. It goes past his outside edge and then there's a sound. It's the sound of bails leaving stumps. It's not a clatter or a smash, but more of a tick, like a godsent swish. It's telling me that that is the first one; my debut Test wicket.

They are 133/6 and I am still searching. I'm surprising myself with how fun I'm finding being in the middle of it all. It's like being Boris Becker, that beautiful stillness and control when the ball is in my hand. The middle of it all being the calmest place to be. Heath Streak is facing me and I find the ball I'm looking for – the magic one I've bowled to Mohammad Yousuf and all those club cricketers. I know it is that one as it leaves my fingers, just like Mike Watkinson said I would. Streak's eyes light up to flick it off leg stump, the illusion telling him the ball is slanting down the leg side, before straightening late. I run towards him, this time the stumps making an earthier, more satisfying sound of a small apocalypse. I glare at him as he leaves.

The next ball and last of the over, I find the exact same ball again – this time it's to Travis Friend. I feel so sure of it and it feels so right that I give myself time to enjoy its flight, to see it shaping in the air, the ball rotating backwards on its axis but moving forwards, spearing and swerving, but totally upright as if it is still – the seam is so straight, so pronounced. Friend does the same as Streak, Yousuf and the other club cricketers; he offers to hit it down the leg side before realising it is ill-judged. It's too late. There are two more: Andy Blignaut, spun around and edged the ball to Mark Butcher, then Douglas Hondo, cleaned up and bowled with the off stump flying out of the ground.

I feel like I can bowl any ball that day. If I was any older or more experienced, I'd refuse to let the ball get taken off me. It's as if, since that first day back in the nets at Burnley, every day had just been propelling me towards this moment, bowling exactly the same type of balls that had been sent to me that day, but this time in the biggest arena of them all. When they put my name up on the Lord's honours board, I have to blink a few times at it to be sure it was there: Anderson 16–4–73–5. A part of me wants to take the permanent marker out of the hands of the member of staff putting it up there (at first on tape as a placeholder, waiting to be chiselled in) and write my name and five at the bottom of the list on Darren Gough's bag. I wanted to be on that bag too.

I was up and running. As I left the ground, I heard the chant again, the certification of being someone else: 'Oh, Jimmy Jimmy,' they all sang, 'Jimmy, Jimmy, Jimmy, Jimmy Anderson.' I felt like I wasn't Jimmy Anderson any more and instead was James from Burnley again as soon as I was thrown in front of the television and radio reporters. I had not done anything but local radio before. I gave them one-word answers, nervously twitching, eyes cast down, unsure of what they wanted to hear from me, just wishing to have the ball in my hand again.

CHAPTER 17

DANIELLA

8 September 2003

ENGLAND vs SOUTH AFRICA, 5th Test, *The Oval*

Series drawn 2-2

We've just beaten South Africa in the final Test of the summer at the Oval. The series has ended 2-2 as the team, now led by Michael Vaughan, has taken their inherited stubbornness, their rugged refusal to be beaten, and are turning it into something more expressive, unburdened and optimistic. Alec Stewart has been paraded off on the shoulders of teammates at the end, his last Test for England played out at his home ground. I will see so many more go over the years. I've taken the most wickets in the series – 15 – and yet it's still hard to understand why any of it goes right and why any of it goes wrong. I'm just doing, hoping, on the crest of a wave at 22 years old.

We are in Elysium Bar in Mayfair after the Oval win. There is a united, collective sense of a Test series just finished, a kind of end-of-school feeling in the air. Most of the squad are here and the evening is cartwheeling over itself in the usual slur of cocktails and pints and the thing I am learning international cricketers love more than anything – not talking about cricket.

My eyes meet hers from across the room. It's dark with red neon lights interrupting the line of sight, but operating in the packs that cricket teams tend to – a code of behaviour not broken by the real-life splintering that other people my age are contending with – we all go over to meet her and her friends. She is called Daniella. When I tell her I play cricket, she says, politely, 'Yes, but what's your real job?' Someone interrupts, telling her that I'm a 'paceman'. She mishears underneath all the noise and in that moment, thinks I am a policeman who likes cricket. I find her intimidating – I'm less nervous around Duncan Fletcher and while playing cricket for England – and spend the evening wondering why she is interested in talking to me. She tells me she is 25. *Oh!* I think to myself. *Is that slightly too old for me?*

The next day, I bump into Marcus Trescothick. 'I met the woman I'm going to marry last night,' I tell him. It surprises even me that I've said it. I have not said anything resembling this before. He half smiles, half rolls his eyes. 'Sure you have,' he says, kindly, and gets on with his training drills. I am in the squad but left out of the Champions Trophy first team that plays out the tournament over the next few weeks. It's just as well because my mind is not thinking about cricket. I'm working out what I should text her. I spend the games watching England reach the final before being beaten by West Indies running drinks to and from the pitch, then getting back to the dressing room, sitting next to Gareth Batty as the two of us work out the best thing to say. I am terrified of texting the wrong thing. One bad move and I could blow it. Gareth proofreads my replies, inquisitively asking when innings end and games are over whether she has messaged back and what she has said.

The next time I meet her, at a pub next to the hotel the team are staying at in London, I am completely mesmerised by her. There is something about the way she carries herself, the way she walks, the way she speaks. I have never met anyone like her, male or female. I think I am doing relatively well just by sitting there, not turning red and managing to make occasional eye contact. I know I am being a bit quiet, but I'm having an internal conversation, trying to process the feelings I'm having. Half an hour in, she stops mid-sentence, interrupting her own flow and says, 'Look, you have to start talking. You're going to have to say *something*, otherwise I'm going to leave, and you will never see me again.' I haven't even realised that I am wearing my shyness so obviously. It's hard to explain that the reasons for it are from being overwhelmed and appreciating that I haven't been fidgeting or thinking of a way I can bail by writing an excuse on a pizza box, or running out of the back door of a pub without telling her. I nod, try to catch myself and save the situation, my mind racing around, collecting thoughts and sentences, forcing them out of my mouth against their will. At the end of the date, she tells me she has something to admit – she's 28, not 25. Nothing is a problem any more. My mind is made up.

Later in the series, with our communication becoming more constant and texts not even needing looking over by Gareth Batty any more, the team go to the Wellington Bar in Knightsbridge. 'You should invite Daniella,' he says, maybe put out that he is no longer required but now invested in this relationship that clearly already means so much to me. We are at the door and are told it's 20 quid each. We are cricketers without whites, looking for change. It's like our superpower has gone, suddenly reduced, the agency we hold inside our world diminished, rushed back in time to people who did things like lose tickets for James on the X43 on the way into Manchester. We are rummaging around in our pockets, pulling at handfuls of coins and notes. As we do so, Daniella walks straight past and straight in, saying hi to me as she does. Everyone seems to know who she is. It is like she glides, floating past me and the bouncers, waving at her with a handful of loose change. By the time I go to her house in London for the first time, I've told Marcus Trescothick again a few times, him morphing from a legendary opening bat to a relationship confidant, that I really do like her, that I think I was right, that this is going to be very serious. I get in her car and, as she turns on the ignition, the music she has been playing last turns on. It's the first Kasabian album – the same and only record I've been playing throughout this summer too. I think to myself, *OK, it's a sign; this is meant to be.*

There is a natural thing that is happening with Daniella, something I haven't experienced before with another person. I'm not trying too hard, shifting around, watching warily and working out who I need to be in her presence. I just feel comfortable. She understands my jokes, I understand hers. I find myself deeply and genuinely interested in everything she says. She is endlessly fascinating to me. Better still, she doesn't know anything at all about cricket. She has had her own career, her own life, an incredible story completely of its own. She has done so much already. I feel like mine has been so narrow in comparison. It is like there are no limits to who I can be with her, at the same time sensing, in some sort of subconscious way, that she is seeing who I am and also showing me, just by being in her presence, what life could be like next. She can see the boy on the bench, almost like she is there at that time, talking to me and telling me what the world could be. She calls me James, not Jimmy. She is not as interested in Jimmy as other people are. It's the first time in my adult life I think that maybe James has as much to give as Jimmy.

In our teens, scrambling around those bars in Burnley, dyeing each other's hair and running out of the back of pubs, me, Gaz and Dave used to say to each other, when another dead end had been reached, 'I don't think our wives are in Burnley.' I was never completely sure if we were joking or not. Daniella, though, is turning what are usually painstaking decisions into simple choices, as if it's the most natural thing to do in the world. It's all unthinking, uncomplicated forward momentum. There is something under the surface happening and beneath every conversation is newness, an ocean of understanding. We are connecting because we are both seeing similar things in each other and filling in the spaces where the other one feels a part of themselves is missing; a kind of dovetailing that is clarifying who we have been, who we are and who we'd like to be.

Daniella is from the Isle of Man, where she and her older brother were brought up in idyllic surroundings. She was not dug into her surroundings like Burnley and had the countryside, beaches and horses as part of her daily world. When they moved for her dad's work to Monmouth in Wales, when she was 11, they inhabited similarly beautiful, rural environments.

Her brother, Nick, two years her senior, was her idol. Everything he did, she wanted to do. Nick was very good at sport too – playing cricket and representing England at rugby at under-21 level. They were very close and collectively very happy. When he was celebrating finishing his A levels, he put his head out of a moving car and hit a telegraph pole. She was called from her friend's house to the hospital, where a life support system was trying to keep him alive. While she was at the hospital, he died at 18 years old. He never got his A level results.

The next ten years of her life, between then and now, she has become a successful model. A window opens immediately between us, where we can talk about her brother, and she tells me she is struck by how comfortable she is talking to me about this and feels like she is not being judged. I know that I cannot fix what she is telling me, but I can listen. I'm looking at her as she speaks, awestruck by how well she has done in her life, and suddenly reflect on how lucky I have been. She describes the period after Nick's death as like dealing with snakebite – it not being the bite that kills you, but the venom that follows. If she doesn't address it, she worries that it will begin to slowly poison her. She tells me sometime later that it has been helpful to find someone who can listen, who is not social climbing or talking over the top and trying to fix everything. She says it is rare in her universe to meet someone who doesn't talk for the sake of it and that, as she speaks about her work and her life, maybe she was running away from something too – her own way of trying to get out and find someone else to be. Her success in navigating life since has been based on impulsivity and independence, and yet, although we don't say it or even know it at that moment, we are both looking for some new version of home to anchor our lives. Maybe she is trying to work out who she is too, without the modelling and without the rushing around to and from the long-term grief and the shock and turmoil she has harboured since. Maybe I am trying to work out who I might be without the cricket too.

Three months later, Daniella comes out to South Africa. I have been on tour throughout the whole winter, not picked in the side for any Test matches. She concedes, for the first time, that cricket might actually be a real job when she sees the size of the crowd in Johannesburg. She walks down the stairs, hears the noise, and has a moment of realisation that she might have misjudged how much people care about cricket. I have bowled badly, but she doesn't care or even know or understand what bowling badly means. As soon as she arrives and joins me at the hotel, I ask her to marry me. We have only known each other for three months, but I don't have a single doubt about it. I've known since the day I told Trescothick, the night after Elysium. I know it is the right thing to do. We go out in Johannesburg, looking for diamond rings as a winter of ushering drinks around, bowling in the nets and becoming frustrated at my own form becomes a secondary thought – cricket paling into the background of my life for the first time.

The only part of this quite complicated puzzle we are piecing together that she does not accept wholly and outright is my flat in Manchester. Around the back of a council block, my parents had found it during the World Cup last year. When Daniella is introduced to it, with its two lazy boys, one and a half bedrooms, a chair that has arms that pull out as a fridge for beers and an old-fashioned landline telephone, she tells me 'under no circumstances' is she going to live there. 'We need to find somewhere to live immediately,' she continues. I take one look at it, a part of my life that could have spilled out over a decade or longer but has accelerated beyond it and outsized it in only a year, and agree.

In three years, we will be married. Around 200 people will come out to Hale, and we will have a do with waiters who turn into opera singers at the Lowry. I have to sell my Audi A4 to cover it. It was another thing that, with Daniella, I agreed maybe I didn't need any more.

CHAPTER 18

OUT OF SYNC

Summer 2005

ENGLAND vs AUSTRALIA

England beat Australia 2-1 in the series

Where I once felt like I was going to walk through the world almost completely unnoticed, occasionally kicking a jumper down to fine leg in a sulk at Burnley, these days my life spills out in a micro-managed, highly policed environment at all waking hours. Drug tests are done with someone waiting in a cubicle and nutritionists monitor and supply everything I eat. On the field too, where I once ran in on complete innate feel, on a wave of subconscious flow, now everything is filmed, monitored, played back on computers, analysed.

Troy Cooley, whom I have worked with since the England academy, is the bowling coach. I really like him – we get on brilliantly. He has me wired up on biomechanics, strapping me head to toe in wired balls, going through my action, filmed on cameras from every conceivable angle. They break it down and play it back in micro-detail, everything slowed down until every step, every impact is measured and enlarged, each imperfection exposed. They discover that as I approach my load and delivery stride, my spine takes on an unusual shape. It appears to morph itself into an S-shaped curve beyond what is considered healthy. It is sent around the staff, pored over and sent back. They decide that it's a real long-term concern for my back. They start to speak to me about the ways I might be able to start affecting the spine to have one curve rather than the double curved S in its stride.

While this is happening, English cricket is fast undergoing a flexing of its muscles under Duncan Fletcher and Michael Vaughan. Fletcher is obsessed with his seam attack being very quick. He thinks, not without reason, that the difference at the highest level, and the way England will finally frighten sides, is to have a pack of very quick bowlers. I am bowling close to 90 miles an hour regularly. They want to find another five miles an hour of speed from me. So, between this philosophy and the fear about the contortion in my back, I start trying to change my action behind the scenes with England. They use examples of bowlers that bowl very naturally quick and we try to build parts of them into me. Brett Lee and Shoaib Akhtar were amongst the two quickest – and certainly most feared – fast bowlers then. I had found that out first-hand. They both have a longer run-up so the staff ask me to lengthen mine. To bowl really, really quick, they tell me, you need to have a long run-up. Other small components are thrown into the air too. I'm asked to try all number of different things. Brett Lee, they say, loads up with his front arm much lower, meaning he can get extra speed and he is not contorting his body as much, putting less pressure on his back.

I am never really comfortable with any of the requests. My rhythm is upset. I feel unnatural and unsettled. Bowling is turned from something that was once the most effortless and natural thing in the world into a sort of checklist, an exam to pass. I am told that it will work in time, that it will feel strange in the short term but long term, it will reap rewards. I nod and agree. I don't want to make a fuss. I want to get quicker. I lose sight and memory of those euphoric visions of looking back up and seeing batters move inside out, that essence of the ball moving late like a laser beam. I forget what I am trying to do at all. Just try and get faster, I'm telling myself. That's what they want, speed. And keep the arm low, the run-up long, the back straight. Everything is off-kilter. When I play one Test on tour in South Africa, I keep bowling short and wide to Herschelle Gibbs. I know that short and wide is the worst place to bowl to any batter really, let alone Gibbs. I get two wickets in the game, both from short and wide deliveries that are hit to third man. I'm too embarrassed to celebrate them. Gibbs, meanwhile, keeps pulling and cutting me for six. My action is a mix of lots of component parts of different opinions now, my head a collection of analogies, scientific maps and explanations. What's worse, the one place I want to be, the place I am safe, the space I have made the world open up through, is now the last place I want to be. I'm starting to hate bowling. I hate even thinking about it.

It's a strange time to be developing a nervousness around cricket, because almost as if they are somehow linked, at the same time the rest of the country becomes wrapped up in it in the most vivid way in living memory. Australia come to England for the 2005 Ashes, and buoyed by what will ironically be the last summer of cricket on terrestrial television on Channel 4, there is a perfect combination of an England side stretching out and reaching beyond its recent history, against an Australian team undefeated in England for 26 years and still somewhere around their peak. I have not been bowling well for Lancashire and am not involved in the series to begin with. The Test series is on in the dressing room while I am resigned to County cricket, trying to find some more speed from somewhere, trying to juggle all the information I've been sent away to deal with and think on. As the series intensifies, I become like a fan, almost misremembering that there was ever a situation where I could have been involved in the games at all, or that it was even my dream. It all feels suddenly so far away. The four seamers England have are a perfect combination of different skills and attributes – Harmison with his speed and height, Hoggard with his hustle and ability to swing the ball, Jones with his effectiveness with reverse swing and Flintoff with his knack for bending important moments to his will. I watch on in awe from behind the sofa when England win by a run at Edgbaston and, before I know it, I am getting hooked on it as if it's another world – one far away from mine. There's something quite surreal about it – watching the England team reach the public's imagination and cricket begin to fill the front pages of newspapers, the televisions of every pub, with games suddenly spilling out in parks and the common, while it becomes a Rubik's Cube to me, almost like a distant memory. I'm in such a strange run of it that when I'm selected for the squad for the last, decisive game at The Oval, I am relieved when they choose Paul Collingwood instead of me for the injured Simon Jones, shoring up the batting rather than going like for like. Where my game is at, I have a sense that I am not going to be able to contribute anything worthwhile and I will be overthinking it, and when the team celebrate on the roof of buses after the final day, winning the Ashes for the first time since 1986/87, a perfect summer of cricket wrapped up, it doesn't even register with me that in a sliding doors moment it could have been me in the side, waving out to all those people, urn in hand. I wonder whether I will ever get a moment like that. I think it might be gone.

CHAPTER 19

FRACTURED

March 2006

INDIA vs ENGLAND

Series drawn 1-1

We are both on a tour with the academy when we get the news. We're needed on the Test tour of India. They need reinforcements, and both of us fit the bill. I take one look at Alastair Cook and sigh. He does the same. We know what this means: it's a full day's travel to get to India. They are going to book us next to each other on the flight, aren't they? We've hardly ever spoken and now we are going to have to make small talk for a whole day. For some reason, at Lancashire we have already developed an impression of Alastair Cook. Maybe it's because he was a farmer. Maybe it's because he is handsome. Maybe it's because he is good. Either way, we have decided he's an arrogant, unlikeable, lucky kid who needs taking down a peg or two. We had peppered him with short balls a few months previous, eventually getting him caught out on the boundary. As he walked off, trying his best to avoid our advances as we ran in his general direction, shouting at him, it didn't seem exactly apparent what was so unlikeable about him – he took it very well – but our minds were already made up. I have blacked out this little on-field interaction when we take our seats on the airline, matching tracksuits, no collective history. I sit down, strapping in for the flight, facing forwards unflinchingly, bracing for impact, trying to invent in my head an excuse that I might not be able to speak for the journey. As he clicks in and the pilot begins the safety instructions, he turns to me and says, 'The last time we met, you called me a c*nt.' *Oh, maybe he's all right*, I think, even if he is a farmer and good at batting. We talk for the entire flight.

When we get to India, I'm struggling to find any rhythm and enjoyment. Every time I run in, I feel less like I'm gliding and more like I'm running through some sort of obstacle course, the air thick like sludge and my brain trying to correct all the things in my action I've done so intuitively before as I approach the crease. Despite this, I'm still finding a way to survive, to do enough to stay within selection, and I'm picked for the final Test. Alastair Cook has already scored a very impressive unbeaten hundred on his debut. I'm beginning to like him. I've dyed my hair red now, as if that will help me with being the new bowler they want me to be, like the red might add that extra five miles per hour and get them off my back. In Mumbai, I have catches dropped off my bowling in quick succession against some of the greats; Panesar and Prior in the field putting down Dhoni and Dravid. It isn't particularly helpful, but we continue to fight.

When Sachin Tendulkar walks out to bat, it feels as if the whole of the ground has come to watch him, as if it is he alone that this whole thing is built around. I have been finding it daunting, bowling at the Indian top order anyway – all of them a roll call of names akin to Hollywood stars – Dravid, Sehwag, Dhoni, Laxman – but Tendulkar is another level of aura. The intensity shifts tenfold and as I start to feel the weight of the millions and millions of TV sets being circled around India just to see him, like you can hear them clicking on. I find another level. He loosely drives outside off stump to me and Geraint Jones takes the catch. As I run to celebrate, being in part fortunate to have drawn a false shot from the little master, the odd sensation engulfs the stadium of total, pin-drop silence. People start leaving. Televisions are turned off. It is as if I have spoilt the party before it had started.

Inside the huddle, everything hurting, feeling this continued pinch of out-of-sorts nausea, the silence and the celebration combine to explain something about the psychedelia of my mindset these days. At least, if I ever have children, and they have children, I think to myself, I'll be able to tell them I once got the great man out. They won't ask how. Even if my body does break soon, I'll always have that. I'm not sure if my mind could have taken knowing I would get him out another eight times, the most of any bowler in the history of cricket. I didn't feel like I was that person then. England win in dramatic circumstances, Shaun Udal spinning the team to victory at the death. We have not won there in 21 years, so coming away with a drawn series in such foreign, hostile conditions is a real effort and achievement.

Despite the constant sense of feeling at sea and inside a different person's body, I am asked to stay in India for the one-day series that follows – seven games in places not used to housing international cricket in an effort to get the game out to the further reaches of a country who are totally head over heels in love with the game. Being on tour in India is as close as any cricketer will get to experiencing what it's like to be the most famous person in the world. If you are a professional cricketer of any standard, you cannot move for being hounded. The level of security and scrutiny is so intense that it leads to a state of constant, fizzing claustrophobia. Think Beatlemania but, when they run out at Shea Stadium, the Beatles are having leather rocks bowled at their heads while people scream. There is nowhere that is safe from public adoration and/or attention.

When I come out of my room, the cleaner wants a photograph, the guy who delivers room service wants one too. I check in at the front desk, the person there wants a picture as well. During downtime, it is advised for players not to even leave their rooms. On the few chances we try, once even a single person notices who we are, it's an avalanche within seconds. If we go to a restaurant, we are bombarded, looking up out of the window and finding a crush outside of the street of what feels like thousands of people, all trying to touch us, shouting things at us, wanting more pictures. Even in the hotel, security is in the restaurant or the lobby to try and stop people from encroaching on our space. On this tour, I am finding it quite stressful when it combines with my disorientation on the pitch. It is a long, tough experience; genuinely quite stressful. I am beginning to learn that sometimes, if you dream for your world to get bigger, and you somehow achieve that, the strange consequence to it is your world also feeling much, much smaller.

The towns are not set up for cricket teams to move through

on this tour. I am sleeping in rooms with fire doors out the back that leave a four-inch gap and let mosquitos in at night. I am wearing a hoodie in boiling hot heat, the hood zipped up to cover everything but a tiny area of my face to breathe through, getting bitten, sweating through my clothes. Meanwhile, as I try to get through a sleepless night, they are letting people into the stadium at 4am to try and squeeze 100,000 people in. Every space feels small, manic, with nowhere to allow yourself to feel at home.

I have started feeling back pain. It's a discomfort as much as anything, a dull ache to begin with, which is not completely unusual. I'm beginning to learn how the body expresses its unhappiness with you after a game. There are mornings I find it hard to sit down, to stand up, questioning whether a 24-year-old man should feel this old already in body, or whether in spirit I was always an old man in waiting. With each town, the discomfort slightly increases; Delhi, Faridabad, Margao, Kochi, Guwahati, Jamshedpur, Indore. We are losing heavily in foreign conditions and despite the pain increasing substantially with every game, I'm taking wickets; Sehwag, Pathan, Gambhir, Sehwag again, Yuvraj Singh, Suresh Raina, Sehwag a third time, Venugopal Rao, Vikram Singh. As I take each one, I'm beginning to not enjoy the wickets as I wince while I run, wondering what is wrong with me and wishing to be at home, where I can try to remember what painless cricket feels like.

Every time I leave the pitch, I feel like the child with the broken wrist who didn't want to mention the agony, fallen on the black ice in Burnley, laughed at as I gathered myself, leaving it until being forced to go to hospital by the teacher. I don't want to put anyone out or complain. It's a long tour and everyone is hurting. I can't kick the feeling that it is slightly unusual though. Every time I do mention it to the physio and the staff, he says it's because my front isn't strong enough. He keeps saying the best thing to do is to build up my front and back. He's positive it's about building up the rest of my body so that my back is not under so much pressure. In between every venue, the hurt increasing, I'm doing old school sit-ups and push-ups in my room, trying to build up my front. No matter what I do, the pain is unrelenting. Towards the end of the tour, the only thing I am looking forward to is the process of running in, because something happens in that run where pain vanishes and I glide through the air, before remembering that when I land on the other side, the feeling of nine times my body weight going through my front foot, I will be back in the world of the living, a pain pushing its crooked fingers through my spine, sending what feels like a disease spreading across my body.

When I come home, I'm in quite extreme distress. I have a scan and it reveals that I have a severe stress fracture, and I have been playing with it throughout the tour, incessantly damaging it each time I ran in to bowl. The worst thing for a stress fracture, the doctor tells me, is high-impact activities, like, let's say, bowling fast, for example. I am put in a plastic corset for six weeks, where I do not leave the house. I am either lying still or walking very upright, maddening myself, thinking about all the hours I am missing, all the players I am now behind in the pecking order for England in the height of their success. The only time I am not wearing the corset is in bed. The same way I have learned that simple dedicated repetition can take you up and out of your situation and propel you to places you couldn't imagine, I learn that the same is possible the other way. With nothing to focus on and no way to exorcise the feeling, I allow myself to slip into a spiral of doom. I'm not playing great for England anyway, I begin to say to myself, so why should I do it at all any more? Maybe I should find something else I can do, something that I'm actually good at. Cricket's not where I belong. I start to fixate on the last year, of carrying the drinks, feeling surplus to requirements, being on the outside of conversations and groups – of feeling alone.

Daniella is with me every day. She listens to me telling her that I don't want to play cricket any more. She nods along at first, telling me how sorry she is. It's like she notices the way a mind can loop a thought around the brain, and she can see me distorting what has come before and what will come after. One day, when it has its grips on me, the same loneliness of the wishing to be someone else, but now armed and teethed with mental self-flagellation, she tells me to stop it. 'The world so rarely gives people a thing they are born to do,' she says. 'And you have it, and you are going to do it again better than you ever have.' Inside the moment, I come to think of it as a pre-ordained challenge, that in some way I was meant to meet Daniella when I did, that I could help her with her pain and, in turn, she is now helping me with mine. Her life comes with a perspective now weighted with the tragedy of her brother. He had a life in front of him, a talent for a sport, and he didn't have the chance to feel it open his life up and take him to other places. It is important to her – then on a sub-conscious level – not to see it happen to someone else that she is close to again. 'Look, believe in yourself,' she says. 'It's so obvious that you are meant to be playing cricket. Soon, the world will see that too.'

We begin to talk about why I love cricket so much, about

what it gives me and how it feels when it goes right. I do not, of course, have any conscious recollection but I begin to locate something planted innately within myself, the same urge to move and survive that had me in a plaster cast until my first birthday, but still finding the energy reserves to crawl. My thought process is turned as I heal, more into a hopefulness, an excitement about what it will be like to play cricket again, to see the ball do what it has been doing. I visualise turning batters into S-shapes again, the ball moving late, the sound of the stumps being hit or an outside edge, the feeling when it is you alone who knows what you have done – that it feels right and that in a split second, the crowd will erupt around you too. While I lie completely still in bed, I keep these things in mind and hope to be that person again.

When I daydream being that person again, I begin to realise what I am imagining. I am visualising me before my action was changed, before I started to overthink everything and listen to too many people. If I get the chance, I begin to tell myself, when I bowl, I'm going to bowl how it feels the most natural to me. It doesn't matter if it is not 95 mph. It doesn't matter if the scientists don't like the look of it. I will trust my body from now; I will listen to what it's telling me to do. You never know, this whole summer could have even been a blessing in disguise.

CHAPTER 20

PUNCHED IN THE FACE

23 November 2006

AUSTRALIA vs ENGLAND, 1st Test, Gabba, *Brisbane*

Australia won by 277 runs (Australia won the series 5-0)

Something hasn't felt right from the start. I am back into the team occasionally but struggling to trust my body still after the stress fracture. The team too is becoming splintered after the 2005 Ashes. Michael Vaughan and Simon Jones are injured. Freddie Flintoff is distracted from his feats of game-changing spells and innings by the weight of captaincy. The build-up too has had all the red flags of a disaster-in-waiting. For one, there's a heaviness and seriousness to the anticipation. There's so much talk in team meetings, in interviews, in the media noise outside, about the importance of winning this series. And yet, it has felt like there's been little discussion on how we're actually going to do that. Non-cricketing agendas have dominated the conversations: what suits we are going to wear on the plane out, for one. There have been endless discussions about it, Ashley Giles eventually winning out on his theory that we need to look smart, professional and unified.

We feel anything but as we take to the field. The 2005 series has motivated the Australians more than ever and – with Shane Warne, Glenn McGrath and Justin Langer all retiring at the end of the year – the toughest, most important tour in English cricket is almost doubled in difficulty by an incredibly motivated Australian team and public on a revenge mission. They turn up sharp and thirsty for payback. We turn up off the flight in suits.

I am standing at mid-on. Steve Harmison has the ball. He caused so many problems in England – scaring and scarring the top order, showing them that England could lay gloves on them – that we all expect him to do the same here. They say that 'everyone has a plan until you get punched in the face'. Facing Harmison is the definition of that. There's a sense that, as in 2005, whatever he does now will in some way indicate the direction of the whole series from here. He begins to run in and – with 42,000 packed into the Gabba and televisions on through the night across the whole of England – I start to walk in alongside him. When he releases, for a millisecond I feel like the ball might have been edged because, unthinkably, it has ended up straight in the hands of Freddie at second slip. It takes me a moment to process what has happened. He's bowled it straight there, the biggest wide I have ever seen in professional cricket. It would have been wide on the next pitch. Freddie has got rid of the ball so quickly, it's as if he is trying to pretend it didn't happen at all. It's too late, everyone has seen. Everyone knows.

Some series have the whole thing, the months of cricket to come, just rolled into its very first micro-event. It was all there. The whole of 2005 wiped out as if it were a dream, in one ball. Playing in Australia can do that to you. Australia end the day 346-3. We lose the series 5-0. I didn't bowl well. It was the same story again. Like all my previous experiences against Australia in Australia, whether that be watching on television in Burnley, sighing into the void, or the heckling of my nameless shirt at the MCG, or here, leaving versed in all the questions but with none of the answers, scratching our heads about what needed to be done to even get close.

CHAPTER 21

HURT

21 April 2007

WEST INDIES vs ENGLAND, 2007 World Cup, Super Eights, Bridgetown, Barbados

England won by 1 wicket (1 ball remaining)

The finger is really sore. I've tried not to tell anyone because I know what they'll say; they'll say I need to go home. The stress fracture and meeting Daniella is now worn into my system, the adolescent daydream of just playing cricket is almost gone. It is not enough any more to simply be playing, mute and awestruck by it all. I feel a desperation now to succeed, to hold on, to be part of something. Anyone who tries to take any opportunity away from me – whether they be staff thinking of my best interests or otherwise – is going to get 'The Look'. It's dawning on me that there are so many more reasons that a career can go wrong than right. If I don't wrest my career into my hands, like a dog with a stick, unwilling to pass it up, I will be chasing it around, back to the same spot I retrieved it from, forever. I have decided to grasp what is in front of me and not let it go. I know what they will say when they see my finger: they will say it's broken. I can already feel that it is broken and yet I am prepared to suffer the pain in silence if it just means I can play on.

We're at the 2007 World Cup in the West Indies. The catch had been to my right. There was such a cruel lack of time between the decision to take off for the ball, being at full stretch, suspended in the air, then feeling it cannon off the tip of my finger, then the pain. The pain is nothing but a nuisance. I know immediately that something has happened that is going to hinder me from playing. There's nothing I hate more in the world than that.

The doctor thinks it's dislocated, so he's trying to yank it back into place. It won't budge. He tells me I probably need an operation on it. There is no way of glossing over the fact that the finger is crooked. It looks as if it's been bent in half like a twig. As I leave the office, I walk across the beaches of the Caribbean, the absolute promised land to play cricket in. I am kicking the white sand, shutting out the blues and the yellows and all the positive vibes you get from such beautiful surroundings. I am Charlie Brown, walking the Caribbean with a little black cloud, which I have painstakingly kept and curated from the north of England, following me around. The next day they tell me Stuart Broad is being flown out to replace me. I know the name Stuart Broad – I've come across him once or twice – but I don't know much about him other than he has long blond hair and his dad batted for England. I am packing my stuff as slowly as I can, still thinking of excuses, when the X-rays come back. They show that the finger hasn't been dislocated, but it is broken, and a bit of bone has been dislodged from it too. Yanking it around was probably not the best idea.

In a last effort to dig my heels in and not be replaced, I call Dave Roberts, the Lancashire physio. I ask him whether he can give me some sort of different advice that lets me stay and play. Is there some medical language that will change the doctor's mind? He says, if I really feel like I need to, I could numb it and try to play on. Then, another surgeon who I have chased for a second opinion and has seen the X-ray, says that there is a good chance an operation won't be necessary. I relay this information like a kid who's just found out holiday from school has been doubled. I tell them the news, excitedly, praying for them to change their minds, let me inject this clearly broken finger every day and play in the World Cup. They take a moment, and then agree. I can stay. Stuart Broad is at the airport with his bags packed when he is told he is no longer required.

Stuart is eventually flown out anyway, for another reason, and we both end up batting in the last throes of our final group game against the West Indies. It's futile in terms of a World Cup – it's been another unsuccessful one, but we both hang in there to reach the 301 target to win the game on the last ball. We are unfamiliar with each other, but the joy with which he runs towards me on winning a token game for England makes him instantly a person I want to be around. It's Brian Lara's last game, four years now since I first got him out in a Test. It had been a great catch by Marcus Trescothick back then, when I was still bowling well before my radar would betray me. When Lara says goodbye here, though, I'm not pinching myself or grateful just to have bowled at someone like him any more,

I'm thinking about the future and a changing of the guard. The future is unwritten, how can we make it ours?

In Galle for the third Test later that year against Sri Lanka, we are beaten by an innings. Myself, Stuart Broad and Graeme Swann are left out of the team. None of us are happy to be left out and, as we are running drinks to and from the field, getting on to the pitch as substitute fielders when needed, we try to find ways of making the day go quicker. When we are not needed, we play guess the song on the speakers, giving each other ten seconds to guess what song someone else is playing. There are quizzes and singing along while the team is getting soundly beaten. The team analyst, not joining in with it, informs Peter Moores that we haven't been taking our jobs seriously enough. Afterwards, in the team debrief, we are singled out and told we are to blame for the defeat. It's quite a thing to tell three people like us, desperate to play for England and growing into ourselves, convinced we can see a future in which England are more successful than ever. A little loyalty is formed between us – outsiders who are trying to get in.

CHAPTER 22

CHANGING OF THE GUARD

13 March 2008

NEW ZEALAND vs ENGLAND, 2nd Test, *Basin Reserve, Wellington*

England won by 126 runs

We have lost the week before in New Zealand and the press have been out for blood. I hadn't played and neither had Stuart Broad. I'd been in Auckland while the team were playing in Hamilton. They had asked for Chris Tremlett, who hadn't wanted to go. Realising I was just going to be carrying the drinks around, I stuck my hand up. 'I want to play cricket,' I said. 'I'll go.' I got 2–80 off 38 overs, not exactly setting the world on fire, but I just enjoyed the process of bowling again. When I come back, it is to find a fractious and discontented England squad, scrapping amongst themselves. We have just had a net session the morning before the second game, at the Bay Reserve in Wellington. In this environment it feels like the nets are a sort of audition, coaches hanging around at both sides of the nets watching intently, with the body language and whispering as if they are picking the team on what they are seeing there and then.

As the new coach Peter Moores calls players in to tell them the news, many leave stone-faced, kicking the ground or wincing into the distance. When it's the bowlers' turn – always last – I enter and those selected are reeled off in batting order. Broad, Sidebottom, Panesar, Anderson. There's a silence after it, like a machete has sliced through time itself, marking a difference between then (up until a minute ago) and now. Peter Moores even leaves a slightly stunned silence for himself at the end of the list of names, almost half-impressed and half-shocked about what he'd just managed to force out of his mouth. Dropping Steve Harmison and Matthew Hoggard was barely thinkable. I am careful not to catch anyone's eyes when I leave to join the squad, not the very young Stuart Broad's to my right, or the legendary Hoggard and Harmison to my left. I don't know Stuart well yet. Aside from meeting him at the World Cup last year, we'd shared a moment when, against all odds, we'd won a game there with the bat. I remember seeing that striking blond hair and bottomless blue eyes staring back at me, and thinking, *God, she's beautiful*. We get back into the nets, the hammer blow just dealt, and we are sheepishly ushered into the first team net, Hoggard and Harmison in the other. Steve Harmison does not say anything to us, he just gets a ball and runs in as fast as he can at the poor squad batters at the other end. I'd hardly ever seen him bowl so quickly. He made his thoughts about it all known without having to say a single word.

In 1855, an unexpected earthquake in Wellington left enough flattened-out ground to build a cricket pitch. Between two mountains – Mount Victoria and Mount Cook – it left, by a strange quirk of nature, a dug-in valley that fitted a cricket pitch almost perfectly. The natural sun trap it created protected the ground amongst extremely high winds. At first a swampy marshland, the prisoners in the barracks next to Mount Cook were sent for labour and drained and flattened it, in time calling it the 'Basin Reserve'. It was slowly carved, painstakingly and lovingly into a cricket pitch – hosting games since 1868.

We bat first on day one and, having just watched us bat all day, I run on to the outfield at the end of the first day, needing to release the nervous energy of the responsibility ahead of me and the always sickening wait to bat. We play football after just to unwind. I am slightly full of it, in a bit of a daydream, spraying the ball around, drifting on a bit of a cloud. I receive the ball and, zigzagging amongst batters who have done a day's graft and are more tired than I am, attempt to switch play in one move. I Cruyff turn suddenly. My ankle rolls underneath me. The ball is lost and I suddenly feel a visceral pain. I can't walk. I've done something quite bad, I think? Humiliated and nervous that I have done some sort of serious damage that will rule me out, I have crutches brought out to take me off the pitch. I sleep with ice over the top of it and wake to a throbbing, swollen ankle.

I get to the ground in quite a lot of pain and the staff tell me, under no circumstances whatsoever can I bowl. I sit there, looking out at the people sitting on the grass banks, especially on the eastern side. There is something about it that speaks to me, something I'm familiar with, the way the backdrop of mountains overlooking it goes to explaining the cricket pitch itself; the outside informing what's inside. It has a kind of humility, an unglorified everydayness, being essentially in the middle of a roundabout. It feels right. It just works.

Despite my ankle, despite what I'm told, I'm flooded with all the energy of a second chance. I am strapped up on painkillers and mental strength and say to the staff that I cannot let this chance go. This is a chance that needs to be taken despite the pain. I am going to go out there and bowl. I won't remember the pain, I will remember the wickets. I'm leading the attack again for England and nobody can stop me. As we take the field again, watching Ryan Sidebottom bowl his first over, I can feel again the energy and spirit of bowling a ball, just the sheer potential of it, of watching it do what it sometimes does by divine intervention, carrying me towards new possibility.

The early signs are good. The ball is doing that glorious, sweet thing. It's moving in the air every ball. Talking to me. Telling me that something is right. Matthew Bell is facing and I run in, taking off on the ankle and feeling its last complaint to me until I resurface from the delivery. All those ideas about my action banished, I'm simply thinking about nothing but doing what is most natural. The ball is perfect, another of those that appears like it's straight, squaring him up and teasing him into playing the ball as if it's going down the leg side, before straightening, transforming the batter into that little S in the air, and hitting the stumps. It's the sound of something new. A new start.

A few overs later, How is outside off stump, edging the ball to Andrew Strauss, who cushions it and then cartwheels his hands away, mouth wide open. I'm using the crease, feeling the help in the air and realising if I come from slightly wider, I can angle the ball into the batter and make them feel the need to play before making the ball leave them again. I get a few to Sinclair that he must play at, targeting his stumps, before hanging one slightly outside the off stump, one that he *feels* he has to play at. It's all deceit, sleight of hand. He's gone too. The score is 31/3, the reserve echoing with the Barmy Army singing the song. The throbbing ankle turns itself into a good feeling, letting me know I'm alive.

Stephen Fleming bats for two hours and 40 minutes. He is a seasoned competitor, a great captain. I know that I need to keep going and not allow him anything. At 102/3, I win the battle, forcing him to go at one outside off stump he doesn't need to, fencing it to Kevin Pietersen at backward point. Then, the big one – Ross Taylor. He's playing brilliantly – very well judged and watchful – and has 53. I decide to bang one in slightly shorter, see if the pitch will help me. It does, moving a fraction off the pitch, away from Taylor, who cannot adjust his stroke in time and edges behind to Tim Ambrose. I look up at my figures on the big screen. They read 16.2–4–41–5. Suddenly, there is no pain, no past, no surreal sense of not being sure where it came from. I feel more like this is what I will be able to do now, some sort of element of control suddenly within my grasp.

As we walk off, the Test won and a series deficit overturned, for the first time I don't feel like I am celebrating as a tiny island – a personal milestone reached and a mysterious place inside an intimidating world more real. Next to Broad and the rest of the team, an evolving unit of players, a kind of togetherness becomes us as we leave. We are imagining a future where individuals might not be in competition with each other, but a more sort of harmonious tension might be created.

It's not going to be pretty, I am reminded by my ankle as the agony returns in the absence of the adrenaline. There is always going to be pain and uncertainty, but at least from here, we are going to try and do things our way. I don't think either Stuart or I would have believed that would mean returning to the Basin Reserve 15 years later to pick up our thousandth collective wicket for England. Ten of them came this week.

It is the crowning moment of Peter Moores' reign as England coach so far too, to have shown such faith in both of us. He is very good at identifying players who might be on the outside and trusting them, making them great. I feel lucky to be in the slipstream of his guidance at this time and finding myself at exactly the right time of my career to have a coach with the bravery to make choices like that. He is kind too – to a fault and with everyone he meets. His batting coach, Andy Flower, is really helping me with my batting. His direction is clear and specific, and under him I become the team nightwatchman, channelling this newfound, desperate determination for the team into 20s and 30s, to pitch in where I can. It's six years in, but I feel like only now I'm really ready to start.

CHAPTER 23

LOSS

The day before our last ODI in Sri Lanka, I get a call from Daniella. We have been expecting a baby. The last time we had spoken, she'd had a 12-week scan and everything was OK. We are planning on going to the Maldives when the tour is over – a belated honeymoon and a last moment together before our worlds change. When the phone rings in the early morning, while I'm still asleep, I'm immediately filled with that knowing sixth sense that can prelude bad news. Intuitively, only seconds between the unconscious mind and the waking one, I just know that on the other side of the phone call is loss. When I pick up, her tone is urgent and sad. She went to have another scan privately, she says, because she'd heard that they would be able to tell the sex of the baby and she couldn't wait until she flew. When they checked, there was no heartbeat.

I will come home straight away, I tell her, the desperate realisation suddenly surging through me that I am not in the place I am supposed to be. The consequences and reality of the sacrifice of playing cricket, for the first time, are shot through my system. I am on the other side of the world, helplessly far away. She is new to Manchester and doesn't know anyone very well yet. We agree that her friend, Alex, whom she models with and is nearby with her family, should know. She should call her and see if she can come round. Alex does so immediately and, when they work out the details of what's next, Daniella is told she needs to go to hospital to have a D&C procedure immediately.

I want to come back, I tell her. I'll come back now. She is insistent that I don't, that I play the last game, that I carry on. Her history – her need for me to pursue what I need to do in a way that her brother couldn't – pushes itself again to the front of the list, her absolute commitment that I should not let the chance slip away now that I'm playing regularly again. It somehow overrides her state of mind and she convinces me to stay. It is only a couple more days; the game is tomorrow, and then I will fly home. I say OK.

It's strange how hearing news can suddenly morph the same room, the same people, the same situation, into feeling like a completely alien environment. I have been happy calling wherever the England team is as home – until now. As soon as I put the phone down, the hotel room feels so starkly *not* home. I am so suddenly aware of the compromise of doing what I do, of having to miss moments like this, to feel like I am not able to be supportive or even share a collective sadness that I too must be feeling, but cannot yet. I tell nobody about the miscarriage. I just suck it into my chest, as if I hoover up the cloud above my head and pull it inside and play, while Daniella watches the game from home.

She is proud, she says, after she watches the game. She cannot believe I've done it, that it has helped her just to know how strong people can be. I'm not sure that I deserve any praise – I am just numbed out, running in to bowl – feeling like I have quietly changed inside. White sunblock smeared across my nose, I am fuelled that day with a discontent, bowling to Sanath Jayasuriya – his Sri Lanka World Cup-winning team of 1999 still framed in my mind as a coming-of-age moment, but now bridging a gap between watching cricket in Burnley and bowling at him here in Colombo. He is taking me on, as is his general way of playing, and I roll my hands over the ball, taking the pace off it, a version of an off-cutter which he does not read and, shot already half played, hits the ball tamely to Kevin Pietersen. I run towards Kevin and my team, no smile, no celebrating, high-fiving each of them with a sense of angry duty.

I still have not told anyone in that same huddle what is happening. The only person I speak to about it is the team manager straight after the game, asking him to book me a flight home as soon as he can. We have told everyone about the pregnancy, overexcitedly, and the players just assume I am desperate to get home to see Daniella. I am on the same flight home as Owais Shah, whose wife has just given birth. He is excited to be going home, to meet his child. I listen to his excitement all the way home – trying not to let on that I am upset or give him an inkling of what is going on. Again, I don't know why exactly, I just don't mention it to anyone. I just say I am flying home because Daniella is feeling unwell. It all stays inside.

When I finally get back to see Daniella, I meet her in the hospital. The process has taken a long time and when I arrive, she has been given lots of drugs and is very hazy. The drugs have kicked her into a paranoia and she thinks the nurses are whispering about her. There is a confusion when one of the nurses asks me for an autograph. I feel incredibly uncomfortable being asked at such an emotional time. I am too thrown, too out of sorts, to make clear that it is not OK. It turns out there are downsides to being Jimmy, scenarios that James would rather handle himself.

We stay at home for the next week, cancelling all Maldives plans, and spend some time together to try and recover. There is no cricket for a moment, no outside world, no future plans, just us both looking inwards, trying to help each other heal. Daniella's hormones are sending her into different states and I try and move with them as sympathetically and as fluidly as I can. She stays in bed for a whole week. I do the running around – cooking, running baths, cleaning the house. It doesn't occur to me that part of this is a healing of my own hurt too – that I am also wounded by what has happened between us and this time is almost like a physical exorcism, a kind of ritual to rebalance things.

It's a strange thing to quantify when it hasn't happened to your own body. Daniella tells me that it would have been a boy. She blames herself – that she didn't deserve a boy, she says. She talks about how maybe she was hoping for a boy to fill a sort of void in her life after losing Nick, something that would realistically never be filled. She talks about how she had given her brother money to go out with on the night the accident happened, and that if she hadn't, he wouldn't have been hurt. There are all kinds of guilt she has been carrying. There is guilt about being the surviving sibling. A guilt that takes her to a feeling that the miscarriage is a punishment for something. We experience how one tragedy can open up the previous one, how they layer themselves into your being, one loss re-triggering every other loss from your past too. I try to listen and, where I can, just make clear to her that it is nothing she has done, that there is nothing she could have done then and nothing she can do now.

What's worse, there are no tests and no answers to this miscarriage. Daniella takes herself into the hellish mental loops of whether she ate something wrong. Maybe she was on the wrong diet. Maybe she wasn't exercising properly. It would maybe have been easier to know that we had done something so we could blame ourselves and wrestle back some understanding of why this has happened. It would be better than sitting in the helplessness of this happening just because life sometimes chaotically deals you bad cards without any reason. My own need for control is brought into strong focus through it – the way bowling somehow soothes my anxiety, because everything starts with me and the ball in my hand, the outcome directly related to what I do. I can punish or reward myself each time, understand why it's happened, work out what to do next. I can bowl a slower ball to Sanath Jayasuriya, based on experience and rationale, because I felt like that would get him out, and it would work. It is all direct cause and effect. It is all control – a control that life outside would never provide.

A week later, we begin to tell people what has happened.

CHAPTER 24

IN CONTROL

5–8 June 2008

ENGLAND vs NEW ZEALAND, 3rd Test, *Trent Bridge*, Nottingham

England 364; New Zealand 123 and 232 (following on)
England won by an innings and 9 runs
New Zealand 1st innings: **J Anderson 21.3–8–43–7**

I have never felt more in control of what I am doing with a cricket ball. It's like it has shown itself with glaring clarity in reaction to the world outside showing the opposite. There is a sweet relief to having a cricket ball in my hand. It will do what I tell it to do. I can see it move before I bowl it, see the shape of a batter turned inside out, hear the sound of the ball hitting the stumps. In the third Test of the summer against New Zealand, I am batting number nine. I score 28. Everything on a cricket pitch is tangible, effectible. I have a hunger to exercise my ability to shape what happens, suddenly impaired by the reality of how difficult anything outside can be to shape.

Aaron Redmond is opening for New Zealand. I run in – watch the ball out of my hand, seam perfectly upright, standing to attention, doing what it is told to do. Redmond sees that line, the one that makes a right-hander assume it is straight and can be flicked away. He opens his body to do so and, as if there's an anti-magnetic reaction, the ball suddenly hoops, evading his outside edge, cleaning up his stumps. He is staring back, confused. The sound rings out around Trent Bridge.

Next up is Brendon McCullum – the key wicket. I run in, imagining the same. Everything happens as if it is a choreographed repeat sequence of the last wicket. The straightening up, the wild swinging of the ball, the slightly confused look McCullum gives back, the sound of the crowd. The off stump, thrown out of the ground, even lands in the exact same place. It's like science and art interacting with each other, providing measurable results. It all makes perfect sense, suddenly so within my power. If I do this, this will happen, and this is what gives me value and makes other people happy. It's all so simple. Ross Taylor is soon gone too, a similar ball, this time finding the more acute sound of an outside edge – pure and exact – and reaching Pietersen safely at gully.

Daniel Flynn is next. A left-hander, I find an angle to him, going back in, hitting him on the pads in front of the stumps. I don't even need to turn around. Out. Hanging the ball outside off stump to Jamie How, a fraction shorter of a length, drawing him into a shot, edging behind to Tim Ambrose. Out. Then a mirrored dismissal to Jacob Oram – this time bowling an outswinger short of a length to tempt him into playing at a ball.

Out. When I get Gareth Hopkins out finally, another ball that swings away, this time a satisfying, dull thud of a pad in front of the stumps, out LBW, I have taken the wickets of the entire New Zealand top order. Seven wickets for 43 runs. Cricket has never felt so easy, so simple to enact or been so within my grasp. I would be happy to stay there forever, bowling at batters endlessly, seeing what would happen before it actually did, and then playing it out in reality. Out here I have an answer for every question that is asked of me. Nothing is complicated. Everything is measured. Everything is definable. And today, I leave with my record figures so far for England. We win by an innings.

CHAPTER 25

PIETERSEN AND MOORES

When Michael Vaughan retires in the middle of the South Africa series in 2008, there are only four days until the next Test match. 'It's the hardest decision I've ever had to make, but also the easiest,' he tells the press conference. It is the first time I watch on at a retirement, knowing that it will one day happen to me, but not really believing it yet, feeling the curiosity and rush of the unknown as he breaks down speaking about his family. Daniella is pregnant again, five months in now, and life is awash with beginnings and endings, possibilities and problems. In the days that unfold, Kevin Pietersen is appointed the new captain of England. Paul Collingwood retires from his one-day role too, meaning that Pietersen is given captaincy of both in a matter of days.

Pietersen and Peter Moores could not be more different. Having not done it himself at the highest level, as well as being handicapped slightly at times by his own kindness, Moores has had moments of struggling to earn the entire respect of the dressing room. I feel this is unfair, but it is something that is often thick in the air. He will stay up through the night, working out strategies, and first thing in the morning be full of ideas and enthusiasm about bowling plans. Everything he says makes sense, but I am reaching a time in my career when I don't feel like I need too much input, and sometimes I feel it has the potential to cloud minds.

His approach, a real dedication and desperation to prove he is doing everything he could to make the team successful, is opposed to Pietersen, who, as brilliant as he is, we always feel has his own agenda. The partnership, over the next few months, unfolds exactly as the dressing room fears. They are not successful, struggling in games, and when we go home from India because of the Mumbai terrorist attacks, Kevin phones us all saying he thinks we should go back, that it is in the best interests of the global game. He tells us all independently that it is not, by any means, anything to do with the fact he'd like an IPL contract and going back would help that.

When we arrive back in Mumbai, Pietersen calls a meeting with the team in which he suddenly then admits that the IPL is in part a reason for us going back to play. Moores and Pietersen, so diametrically opposed in their methods and motives, become locked in a power struggle. Both men are quite stubborn, and by 6 January the Pietersen and Moores soap opera of unrest spills out into the media and comes to an end even quicker than many of us imagined. Both are sacked, opening a vacuum for a new beginning in English cricket.

The whole of the game feels like it's in a state of flux. A match is arranged against the West Indies, playing under the name 'Stanford Superstars'. It is arranged by the Texan billionaire

Allen Stanford and approved by the ECB to try and appease the growing hunger of players to be involved in the lucrative IPL. They're offering a million pounds a player in a winner-takes-all situation. We lose the game and Stanford is discredited and eventually convicted of fraud.

CHAPTER 26

LOLA

This time, I am around. It is a coincidence, a happy accident balanced against England's touring schedule, but one I am incredibly grateful for. The pregnancy has happened this time without too much alarm – a huge amount of fretting and worry, of course – but everything has happened smoothly. Daniella doesn't want to go to the hospital too soon. The events of last year have not lived well with either of us and she would rather not suffer the panic and the paranoia she had last time.

As the time comes closer and closer, I am panicking that our daughter is going to be born at home, and I'm going to be delivering her. Eventually I talk Daniella into going to the hospital. I drive her in on the evening of 7 January 2009, when she is 5cm dilated. It's too late for pain relief. She doesn't want gas and air and is in labour for eight hours. She's in absolute agony, screaming in the hospital. I'm in complete awe of her, the way she is dealing with it, but occasionally slightly also over-aware and self-conscious of how loud she is screaming.

I may or may not, at one point in the barrage of agony, ask her, very gently, to 'sshhhhh'. As soon as I do it, I know I will regret it for the rest of my life. In time, it will be funny to Daniella, but it is not now. The labour is absolutely excruciating and I'm doing my best to be there for her, taking a mental note that the shushing is not the best approach, and constantly working out what I should and shouldn't be saying or doing. Compared to playing Test cricket for England, this is the absolute unknown, a total terror, where I'm completely at sea.

Daniella eventually gives birth to Lola at 4am on the morning of 8 January. When she holds her in her arms for the first time, she looks at her and says, 'I want another one.' I am astounded, given what she has just been through. But, despite being confused that she wants to go through it all again, I do understand exactly what she means. When I am passed Lola, something washes over me. Our lives are new, not entirely our own any more. Rather than it provoking panic, I feel very calm. It seems extremely natural to be holding Lola, and a side of me which is not often encouraged – a gentleness, a caring, a nurturing of something else – is opened.

When I have to leave again two weeks later, I am devastated. I don't want to go. It's the first time I've ever not wanted to leave to play cricket for England. Eventually I have to, and join the first series under new captain and coach, Andrew Strauss and Andy Flower, against the West Indies. We are beaten – shocked by some spells of inspired bowling by Jerome Taylor – and when I come home, I find that Daniella, having never held a child before we had one, has developed a hard-fought routine with Lola. I join in, trying not to break their patterns, and we spend every day driving around endlessly, listening to Baby Einstein nursery rhymes, speaking as quietly as we can to send Lola off to sleep. It's the only way she will nod off. It takes hours, and when that doesn't work, we sing to her until it does.

CHAPTER 27

MONTY AND ME

12 July 2009

ENGLAND vs AUSTRALIA, 1st Test, *Sophia Gardens, Cardiff*

England 435 and 252/9; Australia 674/6 dec.

Match Drawn

2nd innings: **J Anderson 21 not out**

There is the silence of 16,000 people. And to add to the funereal backdrop, appearing out of the pavilion, separating from the collection and blur of bodies and eventually coming into focus – his figure so distinctly and identifiably him – Monty Panesar is walking towards me. Even from this distance, as he walks over the rope and past the Australian fielders, I can see his eyes are extremely wide and wired. He looks like he's been awake for days, as if he may have been in a padded room, single-handedly trying to solve some sort of conspiracy theory. He doesn't seem to really know where he is – a look of genuine, startled fear pressing itself on him. As he approaches, he jogs for a second, his legs tied and slightly buckling over each other like a newborn deer.

We touch gloves. It's the touch of two people pretending. We've seen batters do this, the touch. It's a statement of control. It says 'we've got this' when we really cannot in any stretch of the imagination be sure that we've got this. There are 11.3 overs to survive the first Ashes Test of the summer. It's just me and Monty between the Australians and victory. The very fact Monty is batting below me in the batting order tells a story to everyone, us included, that the likelihood of us surviving is close to nil. Neither of us has history of pulling off anything remotely close to this. Our eyes meet like torches in the dark and we just stare at each other for a second.

'Look, eventually we'll get out,' I say. Monty nods, half-smiles, the kind of smile that forces itself on to your face against your will when confusion and fear are uncontainable. 'Let's just try our best.' He nods again, the smile giving way to a half-frown. It's not just about survival. There are equations at play. We are six runs behind with one wicket left, meaning that if we get ahead of them by enough, we might not allow them time to bat again and save the game that way. All that is a long way away, though. All it is worth reiterating is that this is clearly doomed. Let's try. David Lloyd on commentary, unknown to me, has just told the millions tuning in, 'If England needed a hero, here's Monty Panesar. What a monumental job him and James Anderson have to do for England.'

I am used to the feeling of being out there when we lose. I know how this pans out. I know that no one expects us to do this now. I actually prefer it out here to sitting in the dressing room. It's the nervous energy that's building towards me now that I hate, like waiting to be slapped in the face, knowing it's going to happen and just not knowing when. All sorts of superstitions have played out while I'm waiting, watching Paul Collingwood's rearguard. When I left to join him at the crease, there were people, eyes down, sitting in their lucky spot. There were others throwing a tennis ball against a wall as if in a trauma response. It's like no one believes that without divine intervention, I will get through it. And to be honest, I can't blame them.

For his first ball, Monty offers the face of his sponsorless bat in an earnest defensive shot to Peter Siddle. As the ball rushes past, the bat itself flickers left and right, as if it's a gate that has been swung open by a light breeze. The ball misses everything, including the stumps. Monty survives one. It's going to be a long 11.2 overs. There are two separate challenges from either end for both of us – Peter Siddle, bowling fast from one, and Nathan Hauritz, turning the ball out of five-day-old footmarks, from the other. Siddle is running in, spitting, angry, frenzied, his teeth looking strangely more sharpened, his necklace tight against his throat, like a sort of war decoration. Hauritz meanwhile just probes and probes, trying to make us guess the difference between playing and leaving. I hide my bat in fraction-of-a-second judgement calls when the ball spins, and, at other times, rush to smother the straighter ones. We just about survive each ball for the next ten minutes.

In a bizarre flood of unusual calm, time stretching into a blur now, we are somehow getting closer. The sensation surrounding us changes from foregone conclusion to vague possibility. As we inch closer, the reality hits me that maybe for the first time in my life I am the senior batter in this situation. It is my job to read the situation, protect the strike, shepherd a country home. A feeling of make-believe becoming reality fills me; a ghost of a childhood memory of dreaming about being in this situation as I played against the garage back home. It's all down to *me*. I begin to give Monty more specific, precise instructions. 'Make sure you watch the ball,' I'm telling him again and again before Siddle bowls. 'If it's short, make sure your hands are down, and just let it hit you. If it's full and straight, make sure your bat is there.' Nathan Hauritz is finding those foot holes, causing the ball to spit and turn away from both our bats. 'Protect the stumps,' I tell Monty, with the air of someone whose highest score is more than 49 not out off 50 overs for Burnley Cricket Club, 'and if it's outside and spinning, leave it alone.' It's unclear, to both of us, whether I am telling myself this or Monty, but he nods dutifully, the puzzled smile now gone, a sense of purpose now occupying his body language.

There is a harnessing, supportive energy suddenly emerging, an excitement of watching something unexpected, every single ball receiving a deathly silence before the bowler runs in. Once survived, it is cheered, celebrated, whooped and praised to the heavens before the silence descends again. It's a rush to suddenly have every block or leave celebrated. It's like, as I have grown accustomed to Test cricket occasionally gifting me, the outside is aligning with the inside, my usual internal monologue for surviving even one ball now sharing the same rapture outside it too.

While it happens, I begin to feel deep admiration and affection for Monty. His path to this moment is as unlikely as mine and in a moment of understanding this too, the Welsh crowd are now singing my song but changing the words to his name. We are quietly coming to understand something as we block

My mum was always so encouraging of my sporting ambitions.

I had so many sports heroes, especially Daley Thompson and Boris Becker. I was constantly watching sports stars on TV and trying to be like them.

My dad helped fire my competitive spirit – both of us hated losing.

Above: I was the smallest kid in the class when I was younger, but I was desperate to play on every team.

Right: This is me in the early years at Lancashire – the hair became a bit of a trademark!

The morning after I met Daniella, I told my teammate I'd met the woman I was going to marry.

The start of many years batting with Broady.

My ODI debut against Australia in 2002 –
I didn't even have my name on my shirt!

Returning to the side in New Zealand,
2008.

© Hamish Blair / Getty

Each time I've played in the Ashes has been totally unforgettable. It's brought some of the most incredible moments of my career, including surviving with Monty in 2009 *(above)*, winning the Ashes in Australia for the first time in 24 years *(right)*, and delivering the match-winning ball at Trent Bridge in 2013 *(below)*.

Above: This was one of the toughest moments of my career – losing against Sri Lanka in the final over of a Test match in 2014. That's me bent double in anguish.

Right: Our five days of SAS-style training in Bavaria totally transformed us as a team.

Me, Cooky and Swanny taking a well-earned nap.

Above: Me and Ben Duckett in Pakistan – this was the first year under Ben Stokes's captaincy.

Below: In the zone on the way to my highest batting score of 81 against India.

Below: My family have always been my biggest support: Daniella, Lola, Ruby, Dad and Mum.

In the nets at the base of the Himalayas! Through practice and psychological work I have honed switching between emotional warrior mode and cold assassin mode.

The day of Broady's retirement – even as I watched my old friend leave, I didn't believe I would ever end my own England career.

© Alex Davidson / Getty

Me and the *Tailenders* gang: Greg, Felix, Mattchin and Sharky. What started as a seven-episode bit of fun has turned into a seven year adventure.

My final time heading out to bat. After 21 years, 188 Tests and 704 wickets, this is how it ended.

© Josh Shinner

and shrug and survive. We sit inside a transformation that sport can occasionally impact on a person, whether they are willing or otherwise. We are learning, through the sheer calamity of the situation, that we are capable of more than we, or anyone else, would have thought possible. Monty is very calm too. There is no supernatural, other-worldly talent that is dragging me towards this, no special skill or thoughtless magic that occurs. This is sheer, slightly timid, everyday denial. With each successful one, the blocks gather some Hollywood momentum, our survival developing a little panache – some high elbows, some holding of the pose.

While this is happening, I am trying to read the game situation. It's quite confusing. Obviously if we can last, we can rescue the draw. But, the other survival path is to go past the Australian total and then bat out for long enough that there isn't time for them to bat again. The umpires are clearly trying to work it out on the hop, just as we are. Both their watches are checked and then aligned with the big clock at Sophia Gardens. I ask Aleem Dar, again and again, what the situation is. There is a slight language barrier problem, and I am finding it hard to understand with clarity when the cut-off time is. I don't think even he knows. Forget it, I tell Monty. Let's just keep batting. Keep surviving. Maybe even, something else occurring to me, we could start killing time.

I decide that maybe I need a new pair of gloves. I gesture confidently to the dressing room. New gloves please. Twelfth man Bilal Shafayat runs on with jumpers and gloves. I'm not even sure whose gloves they are, but they are definitely not mine. I only own this pair I've got on. I decide I don't need new gloves, actually. Bilal confirms the time to me – bat until ten to seven.

'Got it,' I tell him, before realising my shoelaces need tying again, and while I'm tying them, that maybe there's something in my eye too. When I look up, Ricky Ponting is next to me, scowling. It occurs to me, as he does, that we might be winning the mind games. He is very unhappy. I ignore him and pretend to be in my batting zone.

The second time Bilal Shafayat is sent out, this time he is with our physio, Steve McCague. Steve is Australian and his hero is Ricky Ponting. It's an unfortunate place to meet his childhood idol given the game situation and the mood he finds him in. Ponting takes one look at him, a million more excuses being made to kill some time, and says, 'What are you doing here, you fat c**t?' I don't think it was how Steve had imagined his first conversation with his all-time hero. As Steve leaves, body language bowed but sacrifice for the team taken, I remember the Ponting that had been run out in 2005 by the substitute fielder, Gary Pratt. Watching as a fan on the television, an Ashes series appearance inconceivable to me, I'd seen Ponting shout up to the dressing room as he departed, it had come to represent a sort of breaking point. It was slipping out of his grasp. From the television four years ago to now, face to face with him, I see the same expression, the same anger and panic.

They are all signs that we are winning the battle. I jab my bat down on two from Siddle, face anxiously closed, forcing the ball to race away to the boundary. Australia will have to bat again. Marcus North – a part-time bowler who is in the team for his batting and had just scored a hundred on debut, is bizarrely sent on to bowl the last couple of overs. The Australian field, too, is eerily silent. They've stopped talking. The seamers are resigned, hands on hips on the boundary, no final call for them to threaten our outside edges or throats. Monty cuts North through cover to an ovation that sounds like we have won the series, then a defensive shot with a high elbow flourish.

A conversation in the middle between umpires, an anti-climactic pause, and then that's it. We are shaking hands. The most unlikely of rescue missions pulled off. Monty and I don't even run as it happens, we walk off the pitch to ovations quite casually, some sort of transformation complete. We'd never experience heroics again with the bat, but like my non-celebrations in my school days at football, I walk off as if I've done it every week, like it's no big deal whatsoever. The number of times we have both walked off with dismal feelings, into dressing rooms of hush and hissing, we owe it to ourselves to hold on to this one and walk it off as our own. We take our helmets off and swagger back to the pavilion, like two pilots who have just landed an aircraft that was fated to crash. We learn when we get back to the dressing room that the Australian wives and girlfriends had ordered champagne in buckets when the ninth wicket of Paul Collingwood fell – him being seen as our last hope. Even though Australia play a lot of good cricket, it brings us some sort of psychological edge for the rest of the series to think of me and Monty blocking and leaving, unmoved, and then all that champagne, unopened, being stared into and through by all the Australian families. Even though we've drawn, it feels like a win, and with it comes a psychological shift in our favour. It is one of the only times I've ever enjoyed batting.

We win the Ashes at the Oval, thanks to a spell of inspired bowling that Broady will become renowned for in time, and some inspired last acts from Freddie Flintoff. The same story I have been involved in – the one with Australian dominance – is finally overturned when me and Swanny lift up the urn on the field, euphoric to finally be touching it, only to look underneath as we do and see a sticker saying: £7.99. It was a replica from the club shop.

CHAPTER 28

T20 WORLD CUP

30 April– 16 May 2010

T20 World Cup, *West Indies*

I am under the assumption that I am going to play in the T20 World Cup in the West Indies in 2010. I have played well in the warm-up games and been involved pretty much throughout the build-up. It's an exciting team to be a part of, one with a lot of the boxes ticked, different types of players with great versatility filling a number of the more individualised and dynamic roles of short-form cricket. It feels, for once, like we're on the cusp of a modernisation of the game and ahead of the curve a little.

The day before the first game against the West Indies, we are on the field doing six-hitting drills. Paul Collingwood, his captaincy a part of the rhythm and verve with which we are playing, walks on to the field. I can tell from miles away, as he comes towards us, that he isn't coming to be involved and is instead armed with a task he doesn't necessarily want to do but is carrying out of duty. 'Jimmy, can I have a word,' he says. My heart sinks. I know this look, this conversation, this outcome.

'You won't be playing,' he tells me. I don't take it well. I say that I don't understand his decision. I leave the pitch sullen-faced, storming back into the dressing room, reverting to the boy who kicked his jumper back to the boundary for Burnley. As the tournament goes on, I begin to realise how well the team are performing and that it is obvious I won't be needed. I try to help out where I can, but I feel like an outsider and a bit-part in the squad. My interest wanes. I have an absolute distaste for not being involved, an irrational and horrible one that sits inside me like an alien rage, buzzing at me, telling me I've failed. Something overrides my system, threatens me in a way that I am no longer prepared to accept.

When Collingwood skips down the pitch in the final, shaping Shane Watson through the on side and runs towards the team as we flood on to the pitch, I get that little thrill of having seen something brilliant happen, but matched with the ugly pinch of not feeling like I contributed to it in a meaningful way. I hate the feeling – of wanting the team to win but also the guilt of not being able to celebrate it as fully as everyone else. I have respect for Collingwood though, who made a difficult decision and, with the way it turns out, is proved absolutely right, even if he has had to watch me sulk for a couple of weeks. It was probably a small price to pay for winning England's first World Cup.

CHAPTER 29

DEEP BREATHS

Andy Flower has brought new things into the set-up of the England squad. For one, he mentions during a team meeting that Mark Bawden – a sports psychologist – will be joining the staff and will be around often. His idea is that whereas sports teams have begun to bring in psychologists when something goes wrong, in versions of emergency rescue packages, he thinks it will be helpful to have Mark around regularly in a positive capacity, to help with performance rather than being reactive. Flower reasserts to us, as he does, that we cannot reach number one in the world without a group of players that are the best in the world at what they do, and Mark might be able to help with that.

Mark explains at training that he is going to be around and will be working with us individually whenever we need, whether things are going well or badly. He asks whether he can have a coffee with each of us. I am the only player who decides they would rather not. Mark is tiptoeing around me in the dressing room like I'm a caged lion over the next few weeks, giving me space but trying to find a way to communicate. He eventually braves it, walks up to me and says:

'Jimmy, I'd love to come and speak to you about how we might be able to get you to the next level.'

'How are you going to do that,' I say, 'if you don't know me?' He says it's a fair point and we make a deal that in six months' time, when he has been around, seen how I operate and observed some cricket, there might be something he can tell me about my own mind. Trust has started to become a big issue for me as my appearances for England become more regular. The way the nurses asked for my autograph in the hospital was uncomfortable then, and more uncomfortable as I live with it, and my world has begun to feel like a place where closeness and relationships with people need to have boundaries with enough of my own space carved in.

I'm not the only one, it turns out, that is suspicious of Bawden to begin with. Graeme Swann says, not too long after, that Bawden was like a lottery winner who got to spend six months around the England cricket team for no reason whatsoever. A lot of people move in and out of the dressing room – players and staff – and I have become used to seeing them pass through, occasionally promising the world to begin with, while I dig my heels into the surroundings and do what I can to both thrive and survive.

Six months later, true to his word, Bawden comes back to me. I have begun to get the sense from him that maybe he is not there for his own reasons, that maybe he does want what's best for the team and genuinely feels like he can provide it. I let him in, just a touch. Over a meeting, he does what he calls 'personality profiling', where he asks a series of questions. His observations, when he comes back with the results, are that I am an incredibly introverted and contained person, but on the field, I am, in his own words, like an explosive, aggressive machine. He identifies that maybe I lack some confidence but am also very emotional. He wouldn't want to get rid of the emotion, he says, calling it one of my super strengths, but we need to learn to channel it, so it doesn't become a weakness. At the moment, he continues gently, it feels like the situation determines my emotion – what is going on in the game, a decision by an umpire, what a batter has just said – rather than my own head. If we bring it under control, he suggests, I will be harnessing an absolute super strength.

Before we get any deeper, sensing that I'm not going to entertain sitting down and having therapeutic conversations, he simply suggests that I try and centre myself with breathing on the field. It's five breaths in and five breaths out, at the top of my mark. Once you get emotional, he explains, your breathing becomes really irregular, which sends messages about a deregulation of emotion to your brain, making it harder for you to manage it. I can teach myself a consistent heart rate apparently, send a signal to my brain that provides some calmness. When I feel the ball in my hand, he says, especially if I am worked up, just try and breathe in for five and then out for five again, with the sensation of the ball in my fingers. We don't talk any longer about it but, over the course of the summer, at first sceptical, I have tried it on occasion. It does seem to really help. It slows everything that is happening down, affording me an opportunity to reset.

CHAPTER 30

BRICKS, BREAKS AND BREAKTHROUGHS

November 2010

There is no information other than to be at the airport at 4am. It's not completely unheard of to go on team-building trips away before tours, especially ones as big as this one. Everything that has gone before in English cricket, ever since the disaster in Australia in 2006/07, has been focused back towards this moment. In the past though, an English team-building exercise has had the odd tendency to unfold into a sort of glorified stag do. Andy Flower is a different type of coach. This is a different type of team. Last year, on the first team trip Andy and Andrew Strauss had arranged, Freddie Flintoff had missed the team bus one morning and Ravi Bopara had forgotten his passport, which didn't go down particularly well. It wasn't funny and it wasn't acceptable. The response to that alone has led to a degree of trepidation in all that are meeting here at Gatwick, with the exception of Swanny who, when we are told that we are boarding a flight to Germany, sighs in relief and says to the group going through passport control, 'I knew we were going to the Munich Beer Festival,' punching the air.

On arrival, it becomes immediately obvious that we are not going to a beer festival. Blacked-out SUVs pick us up, no information given, and drive us deep into the forest. We are met by four men who look like SAS soldiers. There is no explanation still of who they are, of what we are doing, or where we are going. We are herded up. They strip us of everything but bare essentials. Phones are taken, watches removed, wallets banished, all food thrown away. Steven Finn is brutally stripped of his Haribo, and no, he can't have them back, no matter how politely he asks. They take us further into the depths of the Bavarian Forest, not a sweet in sight, in complete silence.

The middle of the wilderness submerges us as we trudge through it, muttering to each other about what this has to do with cricket – a season that was intense enough having only just finished – nothing but dense woodland for miles and miles in every direction. By the time we stop, the penny's starting to drop with everyone, even Swanny, that this isn't going to involve alcohol of any description, as they line us up and tell us that they are there to 'break us down collectively and individually'. The groans disappear and, in their place, there is a triggered sense of shock. We are divided randomly into four groups, all of us from now on named by our surnames only (Flower liked to name us by our surnames anyway). Tents are divided between us, where in each group we are set the task of building them as night falls. For five days, we are woken up in the torrential rain at 2am, screamed at, no first names used and sent to brutal group tasks.

Everything is orientated around symbolic bricks. We are asked to hold them at arm's length until the whole group is screaming, begging for mercy. We are doing push-ups off them. We have to carry them with us at all times, rucksacks full of them as we hike through ravines, run up hills. If anybody makes a mistake, complains or does a task wrong, they are screamed at to 'drop and do fifty'. There are a lot of fifties. A lot of screaming. Steven Finn, when told that the whole group will have to stay in plank position, a whole night's worth of equipment on our backs until he finishes his, lifts himself by screaming, 'I want to fucking kill you!' We are pushing cars up hills, doing group orienteering, not a bat or ball in sight. All of the activities depend upon the whole group to complete. Whoever is struggling the most always has to be helped, has to force themselves through. I've never heard 'pain is weakness leaving the body' more times. A lot of weakness leaves the body. It's not about being best friends, it's not about having a great time together, it's about building trust and dependency on each other. It's about relying on the other to survive. It's fierce and unrelenting and in time, those who are really struggling have to work out a way to push themselves through and find a way to get themselves to a place where their body delivers more than they thought capable. I am certainly questioning all this teamwork when, in one of the last tasks that involves someone needing to be on a stretcher, I'm carrying around Kevin Pietersen because he 'has a twinge'.

On the last night, the squad is made to circle each other, forming a man-made ring, and one by one, opponents are picked out to have a boxing match inside. It begins to unerringly resemble *Fight Club* as Tim Bresnan is allowed fair game to punch his captain, Andrew Strauss. Some land with the venom of a history's worth of ill-judged fielding placements he's paying for. Strauss lands back with the punches of a captain whose bowler has bowled shorter than a length he would have liked. Swanny and Cooky fight, hardly doing each other any damage whatsoever. I am finally picked out against Chris Tremlett. Tremlett is almost twice the size of me and as I face him, both fists held in front of my eyeline, the rest of the England squad turn into a pack of hyenas, laughing and taunting and begging for blood. I go into a little zone, an intense space of self-protection. Tremlett is stalking me. I try it all; bobbing and weaving, the odd combination, as good a version of rope-a-dope as I can fashion without a ring and ropes, trying to lean myself up against the pack of cricketers. He stalks me, taking one step for two of mine, preying on me. One gets through. It's a solid body blow, a right hand to my ribcage that, on impact, I absorb with a lengthening of time and feel an intake of collective breath, everyone wincing on my behalf. I won't find out until we get home that he's broken my rib.

On the last evening before we leave, we gather round the campfire. I hold my ribs tenderly, again the child who does not want to tell anyone that something might be wrong. I look up and around, everyone huddled together in different states of relief, some broken in body and some nearly in spirit, and it's as if all their faces look different to me suddenly. I can see all my teammates as they might have been when they were teenagers too – that moment on that bench, that time when I felt like the world had nothing to offer me, not putting their hand up to betray any pain.

Something very out of character guides me during this time

around the campfire. Asked if anyone wants to say anything, I find myself, almost beyond my conscious will, standing up in front of the group. 'One of the things I've realised I really struggle with,' I begin to say, 'is how I deal with my emotions on the field, and if I could do that better, my skill and my accuracy could really get better. I've been working with this guy,' and I point to Mark Bawden, his face shocked to have been pointed out against the exhaustion of the day's work. 'It's made a massive difference to me, so that's how I'm going to go about being a better cricketer.' I wanted to acknowledge Bawden and the trip has been a real breakthrough in terms of the team's relationship with him – on the last day, we go on a huge hill climb and, throughout the course of this arduous final task, I see seven or eight of the team go up to Bawden and ask if they can be helped with something in their game. There's a real togetherness, a feeling of a shared ambition and will, beginning to ripple through the team.

Back at the campfire, people start talking and, gently, different gestures of gratitude in small speeches are thrown into the air, into the fire, alongside admissions of fear and how people are scared about failing for their families, that sometimes they don't feel like they are good enough. I really feel like, for a second, all of it is OK. That sheer vulnerability in front of people who have gone through the same thing you have, to be able to see each other – not as cricketers, and not even as the best of friends, but just as other people trying to achieve the same thing you are, tied together by coincidence and circumstance, suddenly with a deeper level of respect for each other.

Then I look at Andy Flower. He looks more broken than anybody there – a shivering wreck. This had been his idea and he's put himself through everything the team has, the entire staff have too. There's something in that, a shared suffering, no matter who you are and where you supposedly sit in the pecking order. It's a much deeper evolution of what a cricket team could give you and evolve to be, but nonetheless, it reminds me too of that team of adults I'd first joined in Burnley, where I'd felt safe and understood, where I'd been given purpose and value, where I'd really begun to understand who I was and who I could be. Some of the team take the bricks, keep them with them and pack them in their bags for the next Ashes tour to remind themselves of what they had put themselves through and what they were capable of going through. Next stop, Australia. Steven Finn never did get his Haribo back.

CHAPTER 31

JAMES vs JIMMY

As we prepare for the biggest challenge in English cricket, my work with Mark Bawden deepens. We don't speak much, but I begin to trust him increasingly and lean into what he thinks might be helpful. Mark begins to tell me that he thinks there are two sides to me. That one part is introverted, compassionate, cares a lot about people but keeps them at arm's length, hard to read and sensitive. That, he says, we could call James off the field. James overthinks and undercommunicates. Then there's Jimmy. Jimmy turns up when I cross the line. I tell him about how my dad wouldn't let me win at anything and we develop an understanding of how this has triggered and nurtured an ultra-competitive attitude. Jimmy needs to find a way to win. Jimmy is much more overtly emotional and driven. It rings true to me and is the first time I've thought about making this distinction. I begin to realise that sometimes I mix the two people up, where James might turn up on the field and be overly self-critical, become lost in an internal battle or be too soft or kind. Then, off the field, sometimes Jimmy will turn up when he's not needed and be difficult or moody.

Mark begins to talk to me about a theory called 'assassins and warriors'. He starts to say that when I find the balance between emotion and persistence, patience and skill, there is no one in the world who can bowl better than me. It's just, as he's observed from afar, when the emotion overrides, I lose my radar and self-sabotage my skill. The warrior mode, when in the right balance, is in the fight, ready to go to battle with the batter. The assassin mode is much more clinical, where you need to nail a plan with precision, detail and skill, like playing speed chess with the batter. Every super strength, when overdone, can become your weakness. You've got to keep it in the super-strength zone and not allow it to morph into a weakness.

We both find that being somewhere in the middle of the scale is the sweet spot for me. I begin to realise that, historically, I tip over the wrong side of the warrior spectrum when the ball is not swinging. We talk about how, in that eventuality, I could try to access the assassin mode – because that is when it is critical that I use skill, patience and detailed thinking to win the battle. At the end of a day's play, Mark asks me where I think I have been on the scale and where I need to be the next day. Sometimes it's just by text. He will just say, 'Remember you were at a seven yesterday – rein it in a bit.' I just read it, log it, not even reply. Sometimes no answer is required. I'm just gathering a series of methods to help check in with myself, carving out an art form that's now taking place in a way I haven't considered before.

With each step in the process – short interactions where simple things are left for me to think about and reinterpret in my own words and thoughts – I become more trusting and more invested. I am beginning to feel like my ceiling might be much higher than I had ever dreamed before. That if I can lessen the capacity to sabotage or implode, I really could become the best bowler in the world. Mark suggests that we use a tape that I can listen to that reinforces calm positivity, a place I can re-access at the top of my mark every time I bowl. Every ball is an isolated event, an opportunity again to think calmly and clearly, to deliver what I want to. He introduces me to a deep applied relaxation process, where I find a way to relax my whole body, calm my mind, tune into my breathing. We visualise the feeling at the top of my mark, when my fingers feel the seam. It's all about trying to associate a feeling with a sensation. It's about what you want to feel when you touch the ball. We focus on some for my one-day cricket, and some for my Test cricket.

In the tape, he uses lots of words that I have already said to him. In the right ear, these words that I've asked him to use are asserted. *Top of your run. The ball is in your hands. The seam is in your fingers. You set the tone. You're patient. You're accurate. You'll build pressure. You've got one focus.* We have begun to share that we are both into music – his emails having subject headers of Charlatans or Stone Roses songs – and he suggests that I think in an artistic way. So, as an experiment, the left ear tells a different story while the right ear reasserts my key state at the top of my run. *A man crosses a bridge, with a piece of paper in hand. When he crosses the bridge, handing over the paper to another man, he says, 'When battle lines are crossed, fight fire with fire.'* The message is, I already have all these skills at my disposal and, when I am calm and focused and incredibly clinical, I will fight fire with fire and find a way to win. If I can do this, Mark says,

I'll be the best in the world, even when the ball isn't swinging. It's a lovely idea, and it makes me excited when I hear it. It's something to aim for.

I get the impression he is not particularly confident I will listen to this tape, it seeming like quite a reach from the wordless bowler he first met, but every night I do. I begin to fall asleep with the words seeping into my pores, the goals and ambitions baking themselves into who I am.

Finally, we both identify the two cricketers on the pitch who I can really trust. When all else fails, I decide with Mark, they alone have permission to talk me out of warrior mode and to refocus me on the plan. Broady and Cooky are given licence, when they need to, to simply say, 'Remember the plan.' Rather than blowing up at them, wallowing in rage and self-pity, it would act like a key that would switch me back to neutral. Within a few balls, if I'd lost it, on hearing those words from one of those two, I'd be back into my focus, nailing my skills, hitting my areas, finding some sort of access to control my own emotions and actions. On the days we really need it, David Saker, our bowling coach, goes to find Mark Bawden on the morning of play and says, 'Just remind him, he's Jimmy today.'

CHAPTER 32

NEW BEGINNINGS

November 2010

There is a new togetherness with this team. The goals have been marked clearly – we want to do what has not been done for too long – to win in Australia and become the number one Test team in the world. Andy Flower and Andrew Strauss have been great for English cricket. They are a really good combination, understanding each other and how to communicate simple and ambitious ideas. This has been a relief to everyone after a real low and nosedive in form before they were appointed. They have marked exactly how we become number one in the world – giving us the exact sequence of results that are required to get us there. We know the games that we need to win, the path that is taking us there. Though the usual gets spouted – taking each game as it comes, not really thinking about anything other than the next day of cricket – we all know the exact long-term plan and have bought into it. Flower is the most straight-talking coach I have experienced. He tells me straight and exactly as he sees it if I've done well or if I've been crap. I find I respond well to this kind of simplicity. There is something that takes a weight off to know exactly where I stand in each moment. It goes for everyone else too – it's a regimented, organised focus that is created – everyone driven to be the best they can be. They make it clear that if we are to achieve what we want to, we need at least a few players in the top ten of the bowling and batting rankings. They have both pulled me aside a number of times and told me that they want me to be leading the attack while this happens – shaping a team in our image and not what has come before.

Despite this direct and structured communication though, the discipline and the goals hard-wired into our systems, a silliness appears alongside it. Swanny has decided, alongside Barney Douglas, who has flown out with us as an in-house video producer – years before he becomes a film director – that he is going to do an Ashes Diary. Twitter has just been invented and we are all on it, but no one takes it remotely seriously. There's no tweeting out with your team or constant anxiety about messaging in keeping with your 'brand'. No one knows what they are doing; it's just random thoughts, whatever comes into your head, thrown into the ether. Swanny and Barney take to the diaries with a similar attitude – a series of thrown together 'sketches' of what life is like on tour. Bits are thrown together where Swanny is pretending he's just done a thousand press-ups or on the phone to a doctor who is telling him to 'rub the cream all over the affected area'.

After we save the first Test, escaping a losing situation that would usually be regarded with fear and finger-pointing by the English media, Swanny tells the camera that it was 'nice to see someone who runs like Woody from *Toy Story* get a double hundred for England'. I get caught up in it and begin to appear regularly as a sort of straight man, comedic sidekick. We don't think anyone will watch to begin with, so there's a real freedom to it and we are spending bus journeys to and from training, writing ideas and sketches together. It turns out people do like them, and back home the show is receiving a lot of YouTube views. Encouraged by this, it gets more and more slapstick and out there with every episode. I think of myself channelling all the hours in front of the television watching Victoria Wood or *Red Dwarf* or Lee Evans and the days and time between cricket become less days of holding-pen homesickness and more creative licence to be as innocently stupid as we possibly can.

Being with Swanny begins to fill me with the same feeling as meeting Gaz and Dave in Burnley. Gaz and Swanny are extremely similar personalities. His confidence and exuberance and ability to connect with people has a reassuring effect on me. I often wish I could be more like them in public situations, but don't feel heavy or awkward in their presence either when we are just killing time. It's something that shouldn't be rare to find but, for me, really is. With the series 0-0 after one Test, Swanny does a bit to camera, telling everyone at home that even though the media think we have an unhealthy team ethic, that we are too tight-knit, it couldn't be further from the truth, as I come out of the shower wrapped in a towel asking him about whether he's been using my conditioner.

The 'sprinkler' is born, a dance move imitating a garden sprinkler. I feel like I do it on a night out, but Paul Collingwood will later take credit for its birth. We film all the team doing it, even including Pakistan legend and bowling coach Mushtaq

Ahmed – Swanny says the three white stripes in his beard are sponsored by Adidas. Each player has their own version, most are awful, every one developing in each training practice until Jonathan Trott is sprinkling a constant flow of water from his mouth as he does it, making his a multi-dimensional experience. When we win the second Test by an innings, it begins to grow unbelievably popular – people across the country are sending in videos of themselves doing it.

This win also gives the feeling of something special happening that is carrying us all. There is a sudden belief that this could actually happen this time, an away Ashes win that an entire generation hasn't seen before. Alongside this, people at home are able to reach and interact with the team, given a little lens into our world to communicate with us. This mix of the painful with the effortless, the serious with the silly, is beginning to create momentum. It's the first time in my seven years in an England shirt that I can feel something magical is happening. It's like a tide of inevitability has embedded itself in the whole team through a collective will to win. Between the second and third Tests, I am allowed to fly home for the birth of my second daughter, Ruby. I am desperate to be there for it – something in my genetics is telling me to get back home as soon as I can.

CHAPTER 33

RUBY

Medha Laud, who is at the ECB and has looked after me most of my playing career, takes my requests. Everyone within the camp is understanding and tells me that I absolutely should go. I can feel how much there's resting on this Ashes, because Medha upgrades my flight to first class. It's the first time I've ever experienced it. I get on the flight thinking, *Wow, everyone really wants to win this Ashes away from home, don't they?* My sleep is something being monitored as closely as Lola's back home.

As soon as I'm sitting down on the plane though, any idea of a luxury flight suddenly leaves me. I've got to get back in time. I can't miss the birth. If I could upgrade again, swap with the pilot, put the foot down on the accelerator, I would. I spend remainder of the journey trying to work out a way to ask him if he can go faster, and maybe he would if I explained the situation calmly but insistently. The panic intensifies the closer I get to home – the world shifting from an Ashes tour of unprecedented hope and intensity, morphing back into something else at home, a perspective new and exciting. When I walk through the door,

Daniella is there. We don't even get a chance to look at each other. Her face freezes.

'What?' I ask.

'My waters have broken,' she says.

It literally happens the moment I walk through the door, like the whole thing is some kind of predestined sequence of events and working to the absolute millisecond to ensure it all falls together. We need to go to the hospital now.

I am up all night, reading, trying to stay on Australian time, as Daniella tries to get some sleep. I must have fallen asleep at some point because I come to only to be woken by Daniella again in agony while she's in labour. This time I make sure not to shush her. We have all learned our lessons there. Ruby is born at eight o'clock the following morning. I take Lola in to meet her sister, the sister that Daniella said she wanted the moment she had Lola, then drive them all home. The family that I only have a moment with – the four of us who will become so united – is going to shape not only my life, but my cricket in positive ways that I cannot even dare to foresee here. They are going to teach me that cricket is not the only thing in the world for me to live for, and this in turn is going to help teach me to not grip it as tight, to let it flow through me, let it be whatever it is. Thirty-six hours after arriving home, I am on a flight back to Australia to recommence the Ashes.

I have a punch of guilt on leaving Daniella with the girls at home, but an away Ashes series is particularly helpful company for sleepless nights with children. When I am back in Australia, bowling through the night, it's as if they are with me too, I can sense them all receiving the hyper-green and bright glare from the television sets that light up cricket-loving homes throughout the winter nights in England.

CHAPTER 34

BOXING DAY

26 December 2010

AUSTRALIA vs ENGLAND, 4th Test, MCG, Melbourne

Australia 98 and 258; England 513

England won by an innings and 157 runs

Australia 1st innings: **J Anderson 16–4–44–4; C Tremlett 11.5–5–26–4**

The Boxing Day Test is the centre of the Australian sporting calendar. For decades, they have made it a kind of blood sport. Always sold out, every single one of the 85,000 seats occupied, every four years, and it feels like the whole of Melbourne come out for Pom bashing. It's almost as if it's a public holiday in itself, a divine right by now, an event of entitlement that we are pre-destined to walk away from, humbled.

I am back where it began – the MCG – where I have only known defeat. We are tied 1-1 in the series, an overseas Ashes that has been closer than any in my lifetime. It's one we have an actual chance of winning. There is a different feeling entirely to this series. We have laid punches on Australia that have scarred them, leaving them like a heavyweight reaching to clinch, head bowed as they buy time, happy to just receive punches to the body. The first Test concluded with us, batting to initially 'save the game', at 517-1 with Cook and Trott undefeated. I do not watch much of this rearguard, choosing instead to sleep and recover in ice baths, but I can tell from the body language as they walk off that Cooky and Trotty have made brutal psychological incisions.

Mitchell Johnson, in the last Test at the WACA, has shouted from the non-striker's end at me at my mark: 'Why're you chirping now, mate? Not getting any wickets?' I switch off the side of me that wants to get over emotional, take the breath at my mark and go into assassin mode. I bowl Ryan Harris first ball, turning round, arms wide in a crucifix and then look at Mitchell, putting my fingers to my lips to shush him. It has been captured in one, swooping cinematic shot on television. I'm not aware when it happens that it will likely be the defining moment of my cricket career. It's just one incident of many on a cricket pitch, constantly a battlefield with this kind of interaction flashing through it, minute after minute.

This team, developing over a number of years, is at their peak – a mixture of rock-hard resilient cricketers, all bristling with a tension that pushes the team beyond their history, an accepting of our limits and then pushing against them, a collective, ever-increasing will, carrying around symbolic bricks as sacrifice. We bat time. Alastair Cook – a destined great, is in form like no other batter I have ever seen. Andrew Strauss – a leader now of extreme knowledge and dexterity. Jonathan

Trott – a collection of ticks and processes smoothed out into an unbeatable anchor. Kevin Pietersen – the alpha in the pack, dominant and expressive and a figure of fear for oppositions everywhere. Ian Bell – now a fully formed, multi-dimensional batter with the most aesthetically pleasing cover drive in the world. Paul Collingwood – a survivor, a man who finds a way in all he does. Matt Prior – a wicketkeeper with a desperation to win, a fierce loyalty to his team and a record fast approaching the best in his position.

Then there's the unit of bowlers with our responsibilities exactly chiselled, each certain of their roles and at the best they've ever been. Stuart Broad – now developing a knack of taking wickets when they are needed most, to burst teams open with moments like he has just flicked a switch. Tim Bresnan – a devilishly fast bowler to deal with, bowling quicker than he appears, containing and attacking so that even the periods without the new ball are agonising handfuls for middle orders. Steven Finn – regularly bowling 90 miles an hour plus, his height creating excess bounce and a nightmare to judge or play. Chris Tremlett – at the peak of his game, his stature and physique perfect for Australian pitches, extracting exaggerated bounce even out of flat pitches, with a body built to keep going. Graeme Swann – the best spinner in the world, always bowling from one end, never relenting, offering effortless control and infinite wicket-taking options for Strauss.

We bowl dry. I have learned over time to be able to bowl the same area again and again, tiny variations on the theme keeping batters guessing. Unrelenting. As packs, we pride ourselves on getting out of spells clean, not giving up cheap runs by trying to bowl a magic ball at the end of your spell, so that the pressure you have created on a batter is inherited by the next and then handed down to the next bowler. It's all about packs and a well-worn sense of trust, respect and attrition. So, despite losing the second Test and going in at 1-1, when we walk out of that darkness at the MCG towards the light opening out from the dressing room and feel the banging reverberating around the underbelly of the ground, we are not looking 360 degrees up and around at the surroundings. There's a tighter focus, a sense of collective purpose and belief that was not there when I made my debut here, nor for the last Ashes when the wheels came off by Christmas.

Strauss wins the toss and bowls first. I am opening the bowling, the first to take the ball. Before I run in to bowl the first ball, I register how succinctly everything now seems to fit. It's not like that first time here, when my shirt bore no name, Bay 13 constantly screaming at me and everything hanging off me like a clothes hanger. I don't even feel smaller than the space. I'm just calm and confident inside the most intense, hostile cricket ground imaginable. I'm a father of two now, a young family watching at home in the middle of the night. This is just a game.

There is plenty assisting us to begin with, but my luck is out. Paul Collingwood drops a difficult chance, then Kevin Pietersen an easier one. I think I've got Phil Hughes too before a review shows the ball has clipped his shirt rather than his bat. But there is no inner sense of injustice, of a moment forever gone. It all just feels like it's going to happen, like we are too good for it not to. I am taken off and Chris Tremlett does the early damage. Shane Watson is caught on the crease, fending at a ball that jumps at him, edging it to Kevin Pietersen, who takes the catch safely. Phil Hughes then has a go at Bresnan – not getting all of a big square drive and just finding Pietersen again, this time Kevin's legs bent and receiving a quicker one with equal grace. Tremlett gets an out-of-sorts Ricky Ponting next, bowling an unplayable one that asks a batter to judge the unjudgeable, to question whether a ball can be left alone or needs to be defended. He nicks it behind to Graeme Swann, off the shoulder of the bat, trying desperately to pull his bat inside after the fact, as if to dispel what he has just done.

Clouds then come over the ground, like a gift from above, with the Australians teetering at 37-3, the formations hovering low and suggesting the ball might swing. Strauss sees them and, answering the call as if the weather was asking for something itself, urging him to give me the ball, he pulls me back into the attack. Mike Hussey is in. He's the vital wicket this series, averaging close to 70. I run in, visualising the ball that angles across him, forces him to play, and he edges behind. It all falls out of the sky exactly as I have imagined it. He's gone. My arms are outstretched, all inhibitions gone, screaming into the Australian summer. Then Steve Smith is in my sights. My plan for him is to bowl the same ball as many times as I can, the one outside off stump that leaves him in no man's land, and wait for the pitch to help me out, the ball to move off it or an error of judgement. I get one to just kick outside off stump, his shot already offered, unretractable, as he edges behind to Matt Prior. Michael Clarke is the same too. The almost exact same dismissal. It's all so easy, all so aligned, so synchronised. There is no trace of a time when I felt like I couldn't play cricket any more, like I wasn't good enough to do it, chased around by a black cloud in my home through that year in 2006. As we roll through them, wickets turning into other wickets, momentum becoming its own momentum, the MCG feels like it has shrunk and shrunk. We bowl them out for 98 just inside three hours.

It was odd to be inside unprecedented territory, but to also feel the overwhelming inevitability of it all. I watch Strauss and Cook pad up, the dressing room giddy with what has just happened out there, the coliseum of Australian cricket hushed on its marquee day. I know they will bat all day. Some sort of order has been established which is unbreakable. We are 157-0 at the close, eventually walking off a deserted MCG. The fans have not even lasted the whole day. It's the surest sign of victory you could imagine. After play, I'm trying not to smile too much when the Australian cricket coverage begrudgingly asks me, as if genuinely curious, 'You seem to have matured a hell of a lot since you've been here. What's happened?' I know what they mean. There are no words that will satisfy the time travelled between then and now.

The next day, we wake up to Australian newspaper headlines calling them a 'disgrace' and, in *The Advertiser*'s case, 'Aussie cricket's day of shame'. It is unusual to sense the Australian cricket world warring with itself – it has always, until this morning, seemed so unified, resolute and sure.

We win the Ashes in Australia in Sydney – the first English team to do so in 24 years. I end up as the highest wicket taker, standing behind Swanny and doing the sprinkler in front of the jubilant travelling support. When the teams disperse, we sit on the outfield, the beautiful Sydney Cricket Ground, and share stories about what has just happened over the last couple of months – from Bavaria to here. The first thing I do is not party into the night, but sleep. It's been the most emotional seven weeks of my life. It's been full of worry, silliness, loneliness, community, profound moments of meaning, success, failure and ultimately now in my burn out, sickness, but most importantly, a historical achievement. It's the best I have ever bowled, in the hardest place to do it, while the most is going through my mind outside. Sometimes it happens like that – absolutely everything, all at the same time – too much to pin down or make sense of, just the entire spectrum of life thrown in your lap to see how you deal with it. All I could do was cling on, keep trying to bowl well. When I get home, Ruby is a few weeks old. I haven't seen her since she was born.

CHAPTER 35

UP ALL NIGHT

25 July 2011

ENGLAND vs INDIA, 1st Test, Lord's

England 474/8 dec. and 269/6 dec.; India 286 and 261

England won by 196 runs

India 2nd innings: **J Anderson 28–7–65–5**

We are staying at the Regent's Park Marriott Hotel during the Lord's Test against India. I'm trying to be with Daniella, Ruby and Lola as much as I can – switching between James learning how to be a parent and Jimmy at the peak of my career. They give us rooms that usually connect next to each other. The idea is that the players can sleep in their own room and get some rest for the cricket, but still have the family next door. When the Test comes around though, Daniella is feeling really unwell. I'll sleep with the kids, I say. She's doing the vast majority of the heavy lifting with both of them, me being gone for large periods of time, so I try to pick up where I can.

When we leave Lord's on day four, India are 24/1 and tasked with batting for the whole of the fifth day to save the first Test. This last day of the Test is going to be a big one for me, with nine wickets required. I'm expected to do a lot of the bowling and I'm already working out plans on how to win the game. India, too, have come here as the number one team in the world. It's the final part of the plan that Strauss and Flower have laid down – win in Australia, then become number one in the world. If we win this summer, that will be achieved.

When I get back to the hotel though, I realise, predictably, that all the girls are now sick. Ruby is a baby – not even one – and Lola has just turned two. Daniella is struggling with the fever and needs to sleep. I say I'll take the girls in the adjoining room. It's one of those summer nights in London where everything sticks to you and the heat hangs around; off the houses, through the smoke and the lights, fertile conditions for flu as it commutes its way around the capital. I'm holding Ruby as we try to go to sleep, Lola in the bed next to mine, rolling around, restless. I can't get the temperature right in the room. Is the air conditioning on too high? Is it on at all? Am I feeling sick too? Ruby feels like she is slightly hot and I prop her up on my chest as I lie on the bed, checking on Lola next to me every five minutes, twitching, watching the clock, getting back up to check the air conditioning, to bob Ruby up and down to see if it helps her sleep, before getting back on to the bed, staring into the distance, hoping we can all sleep at some point soon.

My kitbag and whites and England gear are strewn all over the floor, just by the entrance to the adjoining door, barricading the room between mine and Daniella's. I am only thinking of the girls, working out ways to get them more comfortable and to help them sleep, but as the middle of the night draws in and the outside falls quieter, now just the sound of occasional cars going through Regent's Park, little flickers of the nightlife, the gear starts to scare me. What if I can't sleep? What if morning comes around and I haven't slept and I need to bowl India out? The more I think about it, the less I can sleep, and the less likely it is Ruby and Lola will. The three of us just sit it out, watching night set in and then brutal daylight come back, none of us having even managed a moment's sleep.

When we get to Lord's, I am panicking internally. The disorientation of a sleepless night is making even the most basic things – getting on to the team bus, arriving at the ground, going through the preparations – feel like a kind of hellish nightmare. An hour before play, I am still thinking to myself, maybe there's somewhere I can get just ten minutes? Maybe that would help? There is nowhere though, with Lord's alive with the possibility of another Test win, the dressing room populated by all the players I now know so well, the team from last year pretty much entirely still intact, all going through their processes. I say nothing to anyone, I just sit there staring into the fuzz of whites being thrown around and players doing stretches and people shouting different things at each other, thinking about the impossibility of getting Tendulkar and Dravid at the best of times, and dream of sleep.

We walk out of the dressing room, through the painful pinging and clattering of the Lord's Long Room, every sound now making an incision into my skull, through the clapping and the hollering of the members, and out into the light. As I walk on to the field, I experience that same transformation that playing cricket tends to do to me. Within seconds, just in the walk between the rope and taking the ball to start the morning's play, I forget about the night before. My body does too. I suddenly feel sharp and focused. It's as if the world outside the boundary is a different one entirely, and I inhabit a new skin when I get on to play.

We toil for a second, trying and failing to provoke VVS Laxman and a majestically in-form Rahul Dravid, who has scored a hundred in the first innings, into a mistake. I am working though, my brain running through a hundred different plans, relieved for a second from the tiredness, latching on to the task at hand. At 94-1, I have been working on a plan to get Dravid into the habit of playing. Every ball has been at his stumps, making him feel that every ball I bowl at him needs to be answered with a shot. I then come from wider on the crease, creating an angle, the one that gives a slight illusion, and hang the ball outside off stump. He does what I am praying he will do: hangs his bat out there, almost accidentally, out of habit. There is the sound of a click, like the sound of the clock ticking through the night, and Matt Prior takes the catch.

Laxman, just past fifty, is then tempted into a pull shot off my bowling. Tendulkar is at the crease – in England searching for his hundredth hundred. His every innings this summer is suddenly loaded with the heavy sub-plot of the ground wondering whether they are witnessing history, whether they are all some part of it. Even England fans, you sense, really want to be there when he does. I'm too tired for any of that, I just want him gone. As he's starting to tick, at the crease for nearly an hour and a half, I find the ball I am looking for. It's a hooping inswinger, freezing Sachin in a defensive shot that he can't undo, angling in and hitting his front pad. It's out. Later in the day, I get one to angle back into the left-hander and the last Indian hope of drawing the game, Suresh Raina. The adrenaline as I take the wicket is like an alien life force. I don't know where it's come from or how it has been fizzed out of my system, but it has, and we've won. As I watch them mark up my name on the Lord's honours board, a part of me wants to ask them whether they can put an asterisk next to this one, a special mention of extenuating circumstances, that I did it on no hours sleep and a fever. When I get back to the hotel, Lola and Ruby are feeling better but, almost more reassuringly, do not know or care what has happened in the cricket either way.

CHAPTER 36

TEXTGATE

2–6 August 2012

ENGLAND vs SOUTH AFRICA, 2nd Test, *Headingley, Leeds*

South Africa 419 and 258/9 dec.; England 425 and 130/4

Match drawn

England 1st innings: **K Pietersen 149**

James Taylor has been added to the team for the game against South Africa. We are sitting in the dressing room at Headingley during practice, two days before the game. The team have been trying to create a better atmosphere to walk into than some of the dressing rooms that we have experienced before. There is always going to be some healthy competition, but we have spoken about how we remember our debuts and try to make sure new players feel like they are not being shut out but more welcomed in. James is sitting in the dressing room, introducing himself properly to the players. We are all speaking to him, trying to make sure he gets bedded in quickly. When he leaves the room, Kevin Pietersen turns to the player next to him and whispers, 'What's that guy's name?'

It has been a problem that has been brewing for a while now. At first, it's just small things, like him not coming out to dinner regularly, or the feeling that he isn't putting the team first. He's an incredible cricketer, at his best, brutal and capable of crushing and dismantling any bowling attack. It's proving difficult, though, for Strauss and Flower to keep him feeling like a productive member of the team as his stock rises and rises. Two days later, Kevin is batting with James Taylor. We can feel that something isn't right with Kevin: he's angry and discontent. As the players walk off for lunch, Taylor and Pietersen building a partnership, KP decides to walk off with the South Africans instead. As Taylor stops at the rope, waiting for him, he gestures dismissively towards him, shooing him to go back in. It's not clear exactly what he has against Taylor, who bats bravely and with good judgement to support KP with 34 valuable runs, but his body language and dismissiveness on the field suggests something that everyone is uncomfortable with.

Later that day, he tells Andy Flower that Taylor is nowhere near good enough to play Test cricket. Either side of this, he plays one of the most exhilarating, brutal innings I have ever seen. He destroys the South African team over the course of five hours, scoring 149 runs, the ball flying over heads, through fielders and sending the crowd into manic celebrations. Little does everyone know though that this is an innings symbolic of something other than sheer expression: it's a statement of unrest.

There have been rumours throughout the Test match that KP has been messaging the South African team. I don't believe this at first as it trickles through the dressing room. In an era where we have all made an effort beyond anything else to establish trust in each other, it seems unthinkable – it would be tantamount to betrayal. As Kevin comes out at the end of the Test, telling the cameras, expecting to to be showered with praise for his innings, that 'being in that dressing room, for me, it's hard', it begins to surface that there is actually truth in the rumours. It turns out he has messaged the South African team saying that he can't believe they haven't tried to bowl to Strauss around the wicket yet.

As we are all told, there is sadness and then anger expressed on behalf of Andrew Strauss, who walks back into the dressing room from his own press conference with all the colour drained from his face. This is his last Test series for England, retiring and letting the captaincy go at the end of this, trying to hand the baton on with the team in an undeniably better condition than when he took over, and this is the way that he will leave. He will play his 100th Test next week at Lord's, where Kevin will be left out, and the rest of the series played out under a cloud, the press dragging the story around as if there is no cricket happening any more.

From this point on, my trust in Pietersen is gone. I don't think he should be let back into the side. I think what he's done is where we should draw the line. We didn't get on or not get on – we were just different people wanting very different things from our careers. He was seemingly driven by everything that came by being good, whereas I felt like my only motivation was trying to be as effective as I could to help the team to win. When there was enough harmony and a feeling of balance, these things merged together to feel like the same thing. It was only when things started to shake – in the face of a South African team with a motive and enough passion and skill to do real damage – that it became clear just how far apart each philosophy was.

It was a shame the cricket became second best because, beneath the noise and underneath it all, as we lost a series for the first time in years, I watched with admiration the South African pace attack, who had worked out how to bowl in England. Our batters hated facing Vernon Philander because he didn't bowl a bad ball and was always on the money. We bowlers much preferred blocking Vern than having to face Morne Morkel and Dale Steyn, who were both incredibly quick, offering different angles and problems. It was Steyn in particular who, for the first time in a long time, was a bowler I looked at and thought, *I'd love to be able to bowl like that.*

CHAPTER 37

CAPTAIN COOK

13–17 December 2012

INDIA vs ENGLAND, 4th Test, Nagpur, India

England 330 and 352/4 dec.; India 326/9 dec.

Match drawn (England won the series 2-1)

India 1st innings: **J Anderson 32–5–81–4**

There is one thing that the Strauss and Flower legacy didn't do – win in India. An England side hasn't won there since 1984–85, when I was two years old. With Flower still in charge, and some heavy hearts at the injustice of how Andrew Strauss had to go, it's probably a necessarily large task ahead of us to refocus the group. Alastair Cook has been handed the captaincy of the Test side and the first thing he is tasked with – unenviably – is the 'reintegrating' of KP. He does it quickly, without much fuss. I think he knows that, firstly, it will be something that will follow him around until he does, and secondly, Kevin is going to be essential in India if we are to have any chance at all.

There are small pockets of groups in the team – as there are in any social group – and an element of different friendship groups, but the atmosphere between everyone is very healthy. Rocked by the loss against South Africa, there is a determination to achieve something and arrest a downward curve. The team is too full of tough, thoughtful, determined cricketers to be immediately jettisoned by a soap opera and a motivated South Africa. There is a newness to the side, a fierce commitment to it on both a personal and collective level.

We know that, to win in India, we're going to have to bat effectively against spin and have top-quality spinners ourselves. Monty Panesar rejoins the team to combine with Graeme Swann, giving us two really strong spinners to match, or even surpass, India's. When we prepare, there's no huge team plan or information about the conditions, it's more about trusting each player to work out their own plan. Mushtaq Ahmed, England's spin-bowling coach, does drills with the batters with no pads on, making them work out how to get their feet moving and not get stuck on the crease. Each batter has their own approach – Cooky sweeps anything outside of his eyeline and has an absolutely flawless judgement of line and length. KP is more attacking against it, always keen to keep the scoreboard moving, backing himself to hit through the off side against the spin.

We do a lot of preparation with the ball before the series. In their conditions, the seam bowlers almost swap with the job required of spinners. I am expected to be incredibly miserly, not let the batters get away and tie down an end while the spinners bowl into the rough and uneven patches, trying to take the wickets. I realise that the over-emotional part of me will have to be contained and this will be about a consistent build-up of pressure, not letting the ego be dented by the changing of roles. I've been trying to watch as much of India as I can, analysing any tiny clues as to how they make it work for them. I watch a lot of Zaheer Khan, who has fashioned a way to being a wicket-taking threat as a seamer in India. I realise that, as he runs in, he hides the ball.

In Nagpur, for the fourth and final Test, we arrive leading 2-1. It's a shock to everyone – even slightly ourselves – after they have convincingly beaten us in the first game. But between us, we have found a way. Cook and Pietersen have scored big hundreds. Monty and Swanny have outbowled India in their own conditions. The pitch is completely dead and giving very little to me. They have offered up relatively fair wickets to bat on, maybe in concession that we carry as much of a threat with spinners as they do, and as a result it's very hard to find life on them. Sachin Tendulkar stands between me and another wicket. I've been hunting all tour on a diet of straight fields and relentless accuracy. The ball has reverse-swung for me at times, as it tends to much earlier in the subcontinent than in England. I have to occasionally take to my role as a 'spinner' with a technical and literal translation, bowling off cutters and leg cutters into the surface, making the batters play the turning ball. Fitness and sharpness has been an asset of ours – we keep going no matter what the heat is and our standards do not drop.

Sachin is the key wicket. If we can get him early, the score 64/2, then it will send a statement to the rest of his batting line-up – Pujara, Dhoni, Sehwag and a young batter called Virat Kohli – that we are actually going to win here. As dusk sets in, I take the breath at the end of the mark, feel the seam in my fingers. He's been stuck on the crease a bit, allowing himself time to react to the ball because of the deadness of the pitch. If I can get one to hoop inside, utilise the reverse swing, it might take him by surprise. I run in, towards the dusty foreground where so many have struggled and we are striving, and roll my fingers inside the ball. It's intentionally shorter and, as Tendulkar goes to play at it away from his body, his feet not moving and then jumping as if to react, it kicks back from the surface sharply, going between bat and pad. He is bent over when the sound of the stumps pierces the Nagpur atmosphere. Then it is just silence surrounding me, bent over myself out of semi-disbelief, hugging Matt Prior's midriff.

It's the last time I get Tendulkar, the ninth time in my career, and the most anyone would ever get him out. MS Dhoni, the Indian captain, would say in defeat that he felt I was the difference. There were about eight of us that accolade could go to. At 30 years old, I feel like I'm just getting started, finally learning the hardest trick of them all – to extract something out of subcontinental pitches and do it against a team of Indian greats.

CHAPTER 38

CLARKE AND THE RED MIST

10–14 July 2013

ENGLAND vs AUSTRALIA, 1st Test, *Trent Bridge,* Nottingham

England 215 and 375; Australia 280 and 296

England won by 14 runs

Australia 1st innings: **J Anderson 24–2–85–5**; 2nd innings: J Anderson 31.5–11–73–5

It's the best team I've ever played in. We have achieved everything we set out to – beating Australia and India away from home, reaching number one in the world. The team still has every aspect covered too – real strength at the top, with a young Joe Root now opening the batting with Alastair Cook, the usual suspects in the middle order with Jonny Bairstow bolstering the pack, the best spinner in the world in Graeme Swann and a great unit of fast bowlers.

As the Red Arrows fly above before the Ashes start, there is no sense of time doing what it must to us. It's all just ceremony and habit now. Although the endorphins of winning have maybe rubbed off a touch, it has now become part of what we do. Between us, the tension and discipline is an accepted part of what being a successful cricketer is. We all have our internal battles, but we keep them internal, and when we come together, it is with a sense of commitment to a cause bigger than any individual career. After all, if you can't find that rush for an Ashes series, then what are you playing cricket for?

We have batted first and, on a true, dry wicket, have only managed to score 215. It's a worryingly low first innings score as we've not only won the toss with home advantage, but also know that Trent Bridge has a habit of getting easier to bat on rather than harder, so batting last might not be the worst thing in the world for Australia. The score is 22-2. Michael Clarke, the captain, is batting. He is the talisman for the team, by far their most in-form player, undeniably world-class, and we have targeted him as the big wicket to take. We have had tussles ever since he played in the Lancashire League against me and our trajectories have aligned, only coming across each other now for these big moments. Both of us are uber-competitive and in each other's presence, a hyper-motivation floods both of us.

The ball is not swinging much so I am having to use different skills. I am no longer the bowler who runs in and hopes the ball will do the other-worldly – hooping late, turning batters inside out into twisted S shapes. It is more of a process now, more microscopic. Things do not come without my conception, but now everything is planned, fine-tuned, evolved, deadly intentional. I have been using a new delivery for me, the wobble seam. Bowling this, my fingers grip the ball a little looser and you hope the seam will scatter slightly in the air, rather than travel gun-barrel straight. I know the pitch is dry and the conditions unhelpful, so it requires moulding, wickets a puzzle to be pieced together based on experience, information and instinct.

As it leaves my fingers, it feels exactly as I want it to. There is a millisecond where, as my head dives down and the ball leaves my hand, I think to myself that it might nip away. The line and length is spot on, I already know that. Clarke offers to block the ball and, just as it had suggested to me on leaving my hand, it moves a fraction away from him. The absolute ideal fraction, not too little and not too much. There is a sound – so slight and acute – that I think it must be an outside edge to the wicketkeeper. As I see the slip cordon running off and Clarke tucking his bat under his arm to walk off, I notice as I run past that a bail has been dislodged. That sound was the stumps, not his bat. I've bowled him. Hearing the crowd all celebrating, pints thrown into the air and bodies falling over each other in joy, I point both hands at the stumps as I run past, in adrenalised shock.

It's my favourite ball – maybe because it isn't one that initially came naturally to me, as if it was handed to my system. Instead, it's something I had to work on, building it up over hours and hours of practice, working out how to move the ball when it wasn't swinging dramatically and when I wasn't bowling quickly, until one day, it just came out of me, as if it, too, was the most natural thing in the world. I began to understand how the body learns – by having information consistently fed to it, failure upon failure, micro improvements moving you towards your goal, before something clicks and it repeats back to me from memory the song I'd been teaching it.

The rest of the Trent Bridge Test is a real back-and-forth Ashes classic. We have them at 117-9 when Ashton Agar, their spinner on debut, arrives at the crease. We have been through all our plans before the game – the usual meticulous meetings on how to bowl at them, highlighting all their batting weaknesses. But when Agar starts to score runs with the kind of youthful freedom that only debuts occasionally hand to cricketers, nobody can remember our plan for him specifically. We start chasing his wicket a little bit, playing into his hands. He is eventually caught in the deep off the bowling of Stuart Broad for 98. As he walks off, smiling sheepishly and to a standing ovation, we have conceded a first innings deficit suddenly. It's one of the first occasions I can remember in a long time where we have taken our foot off the gas slightly and not executed with the kind of ruthlessness we have been used to. By winter, these small windows of sessions within games will feel like warning signs to the inevitability of a team reaching breaking point, but we don't see it then and just get back to working out how to wrest the order of things back in our favour.

In our batting reply, Agar is bowling to Broad with the game finely balanced. In a back room, I am receiving treatment from the physio when I hear a commotion, with others in the dressing room running out to see what has happened. Agar has bowled Broad a ball which has spun slightly out of the rough and angled into him, which he has edged to Brad Haddin, who then parries the ball to Michael Clarke at slip. Aleem Dar just stands there and doesn't give it out. Broad doesn't move either. It's an Ashes moment that you know, as soon as it happens, won't be a single, isolated moment, but instead carried down over time, pored over and enlarged, engulfing the act itself and turned into a moralistic issue. Personally, I think he has every right to stand there. I admire that he does this. However obvious it is, the umpire doesn't give it out.

At the end of day four, Australia are 174-6. They require 310. Brad Haddin is still there – a really good player with deep competitive reserves and an ability to hit a good ball anywhere around the ground. We are the favourites but the game is still very much in the balance. At 207-7, when I get Agar caught by Alastair Cook, it feels like the morning will be quite straightforward – even more so when Mitchell Starc gets out in the same way. After dropping a couple for the ninth wicket, Cook takes another off me to get rid of Peter Siddle with a really stunning catch.

We only need one wicket and we're feeling good. I'm in a good rhythm and we feel like getting the last wicket is only a matter of time. But Haddin and James Pattinson are just starting to slowly build a partnership. As they edge closer out of obscurity, we begin to have to hide boundaries from Haddin, balancing attack and defence, as we try to defend an ever-slimming total while still hunting for the final wicket. Steve Finn then drops James Pattinson at deep backward square.

As we are chasing the wicket, things start to go against me. There are some misfields – a few through people's hands, including one through Cooky's. I begin to lose the process that has kept me so controlled and focused with Mark Bawden. I stop remembering to breathe. I start cursing at the ground, making my displeasure at the fielder show. Cooky has a chat with Broady, who walks up to me just as I'm preparing to bowl my over and says, 'Jimmy,' – he's quite hesitant – 'have a little think about your body language here.' I stare back at him, red mist going through me as he bravely continues, 'Because you look angry and a bit stressed and are having a go at everyone a little.' I tell him where to go. I run in to bowl, not talking myself down. Broady is waiting for me at the mark. 'I'm only passing on a message,' he says, 'on behalf of the rest of the team that you are behaving like a nob.' My warrior mode is now off the scale, and I spit back at him, 'Did you not hear me? I've told you to f**k off.'

Before I realise it has happened, I am running in to bowl my thirteenth over in a row. I have never bowled 13 overs successively. There hasn't even been a conversation with anyone that I can recall, it is just a given that I will keep bowling until we win this game. At the tea break, straight after my thirteenth over, I suddenly feel the pain. Australia, somehow, only require 19 more runs to win. I am cooked, my whole body begging me to stop running, to stop the process, to let someone else take the burden. I also feel the guilt. I take a breath and find Broad.

'You're right,' I tell him. 'Thank you. Red mist.' He nods back. I take the breaths. Five in and five out. Matt Prior stands up to give a team talk and I feel myself melting into my surroundings, caught between a realisation of deep physical exhaustion and a profound stubbornness to carry on the job. Cooky walks up to me while I'm cowering in the corner. He doesn't even ask. I just nod. I think to myself – one last push.

Deep breath. Five seconds in. Five seconds out. Isolate the emotion. Assassin mode now. Bowl the ball I need to. I bowl an off-cutter to Haddin, trying to vary the speed of the balls he is receiving since he is seeing it so well. He swings and misses, the ball going straight through to Prior. I hear nothing, but the slip cordon all jump around celebrating. Aleem Dar has heard nothing either and given it not out. I haven't even had a conversation before Cooky has reviewed it. He has heard a noise. Haddin then walks up to me, saying he thinks he's nicked it. *You think you've what?* He nods, in concession. Then there is the big screen, the tiniest of hot spots, the crowd roar, the overturning of the decision and I am running off into the distance, my whole team following me, a classic Ashes match won.

I sit in my spot in the corner by the balcony in the dressing room. I don't want to get up, I just want to sleep. I am mentally and physically drained, overwhelmed with relief. It has hit me quite hard to have been so high, so tense for five days, so full of adrenaline, and now my body is charged with feeling it all. Then I think to myself, *Wow, the ball wasn't swinging, yet I found a way.* I have taken ten wickets in one ball short of 56 overs. I'm told, just before I fall asleep in a dressing room full of people, cap over my eyes, that I've just overtaken Fred Trueman in the all-time wicket takers' list. *It would be nice to chalk that off on Darren Gough's bag,* I think as the lights close in.

CHAPTER 39

JOHNSON'S REVENGE

21 November 2013–7 January 2014

AUSTRALIA vs ENGLAND, five Test matches

Australia won the series 5-0

M Johnson: 37 wickets for 517 runs (average 13.97; best figures 7–40)

I have seen it happen to other teams from the outside. The shifting sands and natural laws of the universe parting a once fully functioning group of cricketers, breaking them up and sending them back into the world, each with their own list of how they have been mistreated and where it went wrong. There's a cyclical nature to it – teams being created, brimming with productive tension, then falling apart. I've been part of the restructuring, coming in for bowlers who themselves did not want to go. From the inside though, it is harder to detect. This team is one that feels like mine, feels like *ours*, and when something is yours, a person can find it less conceivable that the same fate will happen to them. Since Strauss and Flower picked it up in the West Indies and got to grips with us, shaping and moulding each of us, the pack brimming with a sense of familiarity over time, a habit of focus and culture for winning becoming part of us, we have achieved so much. We have done it in such a short space of time too; a unit inside which I have thrived and felt a profound sense of purpose as the leader of the pack.

The dents in this team have begun to show themselves, at first in tiny moments of body language or dissent, of ten-minute spells of unusual haphazardness in the field, and increased segregating of different groups of friends within the dressing room. The KP situation involving South Africa was a red flag and a storm weathered, but all of it sat within the side, like the slow first cracks across a glacier. In a packed schedule, with back-to-back Ashes for some reason meaning we are straight over to Australia, the ice suddenly races its way through beneath our footing, breaking where we stand, separating us as islands, then falling into the sea.

Of all the places it had to implode too, it had to be Australia. There are tiny, symbolic things that send a superstitious shudder; Michael Carberry's bat breaks, playing a perfect forward defensive, for example. But there are bigger chasms too, inside and out. Mitchell Johnson, excitedly waved off by the Barmy Army on the last Ashes trip, a song invented just for his erratic bowling, has come back with a point to prove. He wears a handlebar moustache – like he's been given one handed down by the Australian greats, making him seem like an ancient Australian Pom-bashing relic made new. Since the summer, he has found extra pace which, even from afar, is making standing in front of him seem like a terrifying experience. Ian Bell walks back after the first Test, telling the dressing room that he was too quick for him. Kevin Pietersen does the same, getting back into the dressing room and saying how quick it felt to face him. We all glance at each other, unsure how to process that he of all people has just said that. If it's too quick for him, what chance do we have then?

I'm out in the middle and Michael Clarke is spitting venom, relishing having an exponent to wreak some revenge and havoc for his country. While I stand there, showing with every ounce of my being that I won't back away, he says, 'Get ready for a broken fucking arm.' It's not the only thing that is said, but it's picked up by stump mics and repeated forever. Off the pitch, the negativity threatens to take over, affecting each player in turn. Swann is told off in the dressing room for not taking batting seriously, for not wanting to face Johnson. Broady is being made a target wherever he goes – his not walking during the summer just gone turning him into a pantomime villain – newspapers refusing to use his face or show his name. Jonathan Trott, too, has been going through internal demons, and sitting at breakfast before the first Test, Broady and I see him walk past in tears. Trotty's an amazing man, in so many ways the centre point of what the team stands for, and as he leaves the tour for personal reasons, he takes the soul of the side with him.

Swanny realises his elbow is preventing him from bowling and also leaves the tour not long after. His career is over and I will miss him, on and off the pitch. Throughout the tour, Steven Finn loses all his rhythm until he's consigned to a solitary net session, not even bowling to a batter, just to remember the feeling of bowling from scratch. All that fun, all that hunger and desire to work, all that collective purpose is, as if overnight, pulled from underneath us. It won't be until we have the benefit of hindsight and recover from the shell shock of it all that maybe we can reflect on the signs being there, that we had started maybe winning for the sake of winning, like it was our divine right, rather than with the hunger and enthusiasm of when we first started.

And in one winter, it's as if a giant machine has ground to a halt. Australia win the series 5-0 and we're back where we started, trying to work out how to win in Australia. The changing of the guard is marked even more clearly when young all-rounder Ben Stokes is brought into the team for the second Test and later in the series, pushing out his chest and fronting up to all the Australian bowlers, scores a muscular, measured and menacing debut century. Johnson's fear factor alone had made incisions into our batters' heads, opened up doubt, and had them playing shots they didn't need to. Stokes had no wounds, no damage – he just came out wanting to be involved, ready to dominate.

We all know that people are going to want blood back home. They're going to say that it's over for this team. There will be lists over the country with our names being checked off and other names pencilled in. I am 31 – not a dissimilar age to Hoggard and Harmison when Broady and I came in for them. I was determined, under any costs necessary, to not be defined by this series and to move beyond what might be my perceived lifespan. I had got here, I had hung on, I had made myself something else, become someone new, and I was not prepared to go down with this ship.

CHAPTER 40

CRUEL SPORT

24 June 2014

ENGLAND vs SRI LANKA, 2nd Test, *Headingley – Day 5*

Sri Lanka 257 & 457; England 365 & 249

Sri Lanka won by 100 runs

England 2nd innings: **J Anderson c Herath b Eranga 0** (55 balls)

It has somehow come to this. Two Test matches, both travelling the entire stretch of five days. Sri Lanka survived at Lord's against all the odds, batting to save the Test with their last wicket intact, the final ball from Stuart Broad edged and falling agonisingly short of Chris Jordan at slip. Now, it is our turn to survive. Moeen Ali, new to Test cricket, has batted fluently, expressively and with courage to reach 108 not out. His rearguard effort, somehow languid and expressive, has nearly taken us there, but as we fight to draw the game with only one wicket in hand, I am left to face the last over myself.

I hate batting. I always have. I resent that cricket throws me into these situations where, batting 11 for England, I am often left in the tensest position and with the entire fate of a series depending on some sort of act of God. It's always me that's there when things have gone wrong. Always me there to shake hands when we have been beaten, the final punch always landing on me. Now, I have to face six balls from Shaminda Eranga. All I need to do is not get out, save the series, stop Sri Lanka from a first series win in England that they are desperate for. I keep telling myself: just watch the ball. Stay in line with it. Let it hit you if it needs to. If it hurts, that's fine. Physical pain is preferable to losing. I know how to deal with physical pain.

Eranga's action is hard to read – the ball tends to feel like it catapults from nowhere, extracting pace out of the wicket in odd moments, causing the ball to spit, often in the throat area. I know the ball will be in one of two places – my toes, or my head. He runs in to bowl his first ball. I am exhausted from everything that has happened over the past two weeks, every mind-bending passage of play and yet, whatever happens in the next five minutes is the only thing that will matter. It will entirely frame everything that has come before it.

My eyes are enormous, half startled, half manically focused, my tongue pressing on my top lip. The first ball is short, quick, just outside off stump. I must be sensing everything in hyper-real motion because I feel like I have almost too much time to watch it. I get inside it, block the ball relatively safely. It rolls to the man at bat-pad. As it does, it is like my peripheral vision widens and a tunnel I've been travelling through has opened up. There are so many fielders surrounding the bat. Survived one, five to go. I take a breath and walk away from the crease to calm myself down. The entire scope of a summer is inside this moment, the crowd holding their breath with me, the sky dark and tense.

I settle back at the crease, the sky darkens again, the tunnel my only focus. The second ball is similar. I watch it and guide it safely to gully. Two gone, four to go. Eranga comes over the wicket for his third ball. It's a change of angle, trying to cramp me for space. As he runs in, I wonder if my eyebrows look as inward-facing as they feel they are, whether it appears as my senses tell me, like parts of my face are being pulled all over the place, distorting and imploding like a Picasso. It all feels so life and death. Nothing could be more important than surviving here. It's another short ball that I watch, surprising myself again with the amount of time I have to see it, and again block it. The fourth ball of the over, I'm convinced that this time he will try to bowl fuller given that he has me going back and across, on to my stumps with each short ball. The tunnel encloses. I'm right, I get right in behind and block it. Two to come.

There is a horrible nervous energy that comes with batting. Of all the disciplines in all the sports, for some reason, batting is the one that I have never been able to make feel natural. I play golf right-handed, I bowl right-handed, I throw right-handed, I play tennis right-handed . . . but I bat left-handed. It's so perplexing that Marcus Trescothick has genuinely tried a number of times to see if I'm batting the wrong way round. Each time we leave the nets puzzled and beaten, concluding that I probably was batting the right way round, I just couldn't do it very well. I expend more energy walking back and forth in the dressing room, waiting to bat, than I do in the field sometimes.

What sort of a cruel sport is this where it will make you

attempt something you are completely unequipped to do, again and again, forever and ever? What sort of cruel sport leaves you as the last man too, suffering the indignity of everyone preying on your resistance while the rest of your team – some of them batters by trade who have got themselves out – have the audacity to watch on, praying you survive? I wake up at night sometimes, visions of cricket balls flying towards my head, flinching and then sitting bolt upright in bed. *Phew,* I think. *I'm not batting. It's OK. Go back to sleep.* The thing I really can't deal with is the idea that I may have let my teammates down and that there might be one tiny moment amongst millions, a split-second reflex response to a cricket ball with less than half a second to make your move, that I will be regretting forever.

There are two balls remaining. The clapping, the panic, the urgency in between deliveries dies down. The tunnel again encloses. It's a sickening silence as Eranga is about to run in. It's the sort of silence that precedes a vertical drop on a roller coaster. He runs in. I know what to do; it's worked so far. Get back and across and give myself time to jam the bat down on it whether it is full or short. He runs in and delivers with that catapult action I've been finding so hard to read. I'm back and across, but this time it feels twice as fast as anything he's bowled. It's the one that spits out of nowhere. The last sight I have of it is as it spears at my face. I get my bat somewhere near it, but I'm not in control of it. The ball spoons into the air off my bat handle and it feels like it is in the air for the entire duration of the past ten days of cricket. In fact, it feels longer. As Rangana Herath takes the catch, giving Sri Lanka their first ever series win in England, I am bowed, my eyes closed, hunched over. I never want to stand up again, to see sunlight again. I never want to open my eyes. I can hear the wild celebrating of the Sri Lankans and then, more gently, the presence of Moeen Ali, standing next to me, not sure what to say. A dark cloud hangs over me like the world has ended. Nobody could convince me otherwise.

Half an hour later, I still haven't said a word as I am called for the press conference with Mike Atherton, receiving the player of the series award. I'd bowled really well at Lord's and Headingley, taking 12 wickets in the series. Not that any of it mattered any more. I just feel the pure exhaustion of defeat, the humiliation of having not been able to see the team over the line and, at his first question, feel myself turning away, unable to answer, tears flooding my senses.

CHAPTER 41

INDIA 81

9–13 July 2014

ENGLAND vs INDIA, 1st Test, *Trent Bridge, Nottingham*

India 457 and 391/9 dec.; England 496

Match drawn

England 1st innings: **J Root 154; J Anderson 81**

Cricket always balances the scales – that's how I came to think of it. If you have moments of feeling untouchable, it finds a way to make you feel small. Sometimes it can take you from one to the other in seconds. Likewise though, if it serves you up some sort of heartbreak or crushing disappointment, one you fear you may never recover from, if you hang in there, you will be likely shown a space for redemption.

At Trent Bridge a month later, the score is 298/9 when I come to the wicket against India, answering their already above-par score of 457. It's a treacherous position. The pitch is horribly slow, which makes it a slight moment of relief for me, leaving me a little bit more time to play fast bowlers, but it has made it difficult to time the ball for most of our batting unit. Andy Flower has worked with me on my batting for a long time – patiently feeding me balls, trying to tell me where my scoring options might be and encouraging me to be confident and brave in defence.

Flower has even given me the dubious honour of being a nightwatchman in the years before. Even though at times I've been able to carry out this duty well, warding off quicks and preserving game situations so batters are protected for the next day, I've not always enjoyed it. It flushes my body with nervous adrenaline throughout our batting innings, never being sure at what notice I'm going to be needed and feeling like some sort of sacrificial target for the game's most challenging situations, usually when my body is already complaining about the workload. Despite feeling like I have surely earned some sort of seniority pass to throw someone who isn't the leader of the bowling attack out there to get hit, I have learned to suck it up. If it's what the team needs, it's what I'm prepared to do.

I am not nightwatchman today, but Joe Root at the other end is in need of someone to hang around at the crease with him. Joe has an extremely calm presence to him. He exudes nothing but a lightness of touch when he bats. From the moment he walked into the England team, the more intense the battle or the situation, the more Joe smiled. He loves being in a fight – it brings some sort of youthful playfulness out of him rather than hyper anxiety. He is beautiful to watch too – a mixture of all the best elements of traditional, aesthetic batting and an electric knack for improvisation and modernity.

When I get to the crease, he punches gloves with me, smiling, and very simply tells me the plan, as if it's a shopping list he's asked me to go out and get for him. He'll bat for four balls, then rotate the strike and give me two balls to face. I nod, my expression complete with the concerned inward-facing eyebrows that seem only to muscle themselves on to my face when I'm out to bat, twitching as I do. For the first of my two balls, Joe's seeming to find the gap at will every time he needs the single and a couple of overs later, I'm already beginning to feel less anxious than I usually would. Jadeja runs around the wicket and bowls to me and, as he drops the ball short, I drop my hands, turn them around, effecting a reverse sweep and hit the ball behind square for four. For a second, the reverse sweep has my hands around the other way, almost appearing right-handed just for the split-second in the shot. Maybe Trescothick was half right? It's as close to a natural cricket shot as I've ever felt myself play. The crowd goes up in cheers, ones I would find semi-sarcastic, slightly patronising usually, but here it feels like everyone is remembering a month earlier, that Sri Lanka defeat still in the air, and something is due to be exorcised.

Shami bowls around the wicket, running out from behind the umpire, and I am punching him on the back foot for four. It feels like the shot of a proper batter. I do not celebrate, or let on how much I have enjoyed it. It's like the goal I scored at school. I feel like I'm not sure where it has come from but use all my power to make it seem like this is something I do every day, business as usual. Jadeja is in again and this time I'm on my knees, reverse-sweeping square. This one's even better. Shami runs in – angrier by the treatment – and bowls short. It sits up nicely, the pitch not quick enough to rush me, and for a second I'm the image of Boris Becker, just like the way I used to re-enact at home with the settee in front of the TV, double-handedly smashing it down the line.

I'm suddenly flicking the ball off my hips and timing it perfectly for four, the kind of shots that tempt fielders to chase all the way to the boundary, but they never reach. When I pass my best Test score, Joe Root walks up to me, beaming, patting me on the shoulder, telling me to keep going. I begin to feel like he's enjoying watching me more than batting himself. By the time Shami's running in to bowl to me, we have put on a hundred for the last wicket, 47 of them mine. I've a sixth sense he's going to drop it short again, so I charge down the wicket, reach the ball from outside my eyeline on the off side and carve it in the opposite direction, momentarily losing hold of the bat handle, and watch the ball race over the boundary for four.

I have 50 in a Test match – one more than I managed in that 50 overs grind for Burnley. The crowd is all on their feet and Joe is running towards me, laughing, hugging me as I let a smile finally show itself on my face. The toil with the ball – all of the running in and constant physical exertion that I had put in for England – finally repaying me with one afternoon where I know what it feels like to be a genuine Test match batter. I am in the land of fantasy again, feeling that sense of transcendence that Test cricket gives you, allowing you to find something else completely in you that you didn't know you had.

It's turned into a Zen-like state by the time I'm continuing to play shots. We've forgotten about the protecting of the strike between us, just two batters playing shots, reading the game, acting on pure instinct, caught up in a moment that once set in motion has no friction or tension in it at all, just pure enjoyment. I'm skipping down the pitch and hitting the ball down the ground to level the scores. I've been at the wicket now for longer than any number 11 in the history of Test cricket. We both hold the record for the highest tenth wicket partnership in Test match history. There are shots I didn't even know I had. On drives suddenly. Cover drives through point. Sashays and punches down the ground.

When tea comes around, England have a lead and the Test has been turned completely on its head. I feel like the last four hours have been an effortless dream – nothing about it gruelling whatsoever. As I'm sitting there in the dressing room, a stupid grin on my face, watching people hang around laughing and gawping at the shots being played on television, Matt Prior comes and sits next to me: 'Only 19 more.' *Only 19 more to what?* I think to myself. Then it strikes me. I am 81 not out in a Test match, only 19 short of a century. In that very moment – as if the pinch of reality and recognition grounds me to earth from a cartoon – I know that the dream is over. I'm going to overthink it now, it's too much to contemplate.

I am, inevitably, immediately out as play restarts, the last session seemingly just a mirage that existed in its own parallel universe. The crowd gets to their feet and I soak up the applause, pointing my bat back at all the stands. We have put on 198 runs for the tenth wicket.

After the game, Joe gives me a bat, signing the handle 'To the all-rounder, love Joe'. I have heard people say about Root from afar, teammates and media and coaches: 'I don't know how he does it.' For one innings, I actually do. It's a joy – a simplicity of expression that you can consider yourself privileged to have experienced just once. Joe had my back then – willing the whole thing true. He always did. And so did the rest of Trent Bridge, the vision of me being haunched over, tears in my eyes, only a month old, all of that made sense of now by what had moved through my system today. If you hang in there with the game long enough, it swoops back to teach you something that's good for you, or repays you for your time. It's all part of what makes Test cricket so great – suffering and joy – it reaches in and pulls out emotions and reserves within you that you didn't know you had.

CHAPTER 42

OVERTAKING BOTHAM

13–17 April 2015

WEST INDIES vs ENGLAND, 1st Test, North Sound, Antigua

England 399 and 333/7 dec.; West Indies 295 and 350/7

Match drawn

West Indies 1st innings: **J Anderson 23–9–67–2**; 2nd innings:
J Anderson 24.4–3–72–2

It's my 100th Test. It's hard to believe the time that has swelled and contracted, on and off the pitch, since Nasser Hussain gave me my first cap. It's a number that I associate with Mike Atherton and Alec Stewart, even a distant memory being David Gower reaching the same mark, three of only a handful of cricketers to have got there in history. They seem like real adults, their achievement born out of careers decades long, legacies already assured. Mine does not feel comparable. It feels as if someone has pulled a band back and then let it go, every Test flashing before my eyes in quicker succession than I have time to grasp.

FINDING THE EDGE

From the outside, it's hard to judge exactly or understand the wider impact that playing for England this long has had on me. My life has been a series of the same day in different places, being ferried together with the team from one place to the next, complete focus on the job in hand before that gives way to the next. It all blurs into one cartwheeling, endless adventure after a while. Meanwhile, a sense of what it means to stay in people's lives over a period of time has come into view this week. I'm asked about it constantly; told that different parts of people's lives have been experienced through something I've done on a cricket pitch. My family have flown over, friends too. If I take four wickets, I will become the all-time highest wicket taker for England, going beyond Ian Botham.

We're in Antigua where the pitch is docile, and taking wickets is as difficult as anywhere in the world. The pitch will not help. The ball will not move. Prising out West Indian batters takes long periods of concentration, subtle plans that take place only with sustained pressure. I have taken two wickets in the first innings and then one more in the second, the important one of Marlon Samuels. Captain Denesh Ramdin is unbeaten on 57. Time is running out to win the Test match somehow.

As I continue to run in to bowl, Stuart Broad comes to speak to me at mid-on. 'How about trying to bowl a leg cutter?' he suggests. I haven't bowled many, and it's not something that has been a huge part of the 384 previous wickets for England. The majority of those have been the subtleties of feel between my index and middle finger, that callus, building up rugged dead skin over years, dictating whether the balls move in or away or go straight on. I run in and try one. It's quite floaty, easy to read, and comes out of my hand slowly without moving.

I huff at Broady on the way back to my mark and shrug when I reach him. 'Bowl it again,' he says, 'but try it as fast as you can.'

It comes out perfectly, revolutions fizzing in the air so rapidly that you can hear the sound. Ramdin edges the ball and then I see Alastair Cook diving to his left, taking the catch at full stretch. I haven't realised quite how much this landmark must mean to me – but it suddenly hits me, all the distance travelled, all the miraculous coincidences, the daily act of just showing up again and again. Cook and Broad are involved too, like it was meant to be. Ball in hand, I turn to show it to the crowd, who are on their feet, and spot Daniella and the girls, my mum and dad, and then, to their right, Ian Botham, both arms up, applauding too.

CHAPTER 43

2015 ASHES BROAD SPELL

6–8 August 2015

ENGLAND vs AUSTRALIA, 4th Test, *Trent Bridge, Nottingham*

Australia 60 and 253; England 391/9 dec.

England won by an innings and 78 runs

Australia 1st innings: **S Broad 8–15**

It's a year later – the Trent Bridge Ashes Test. I'm miserable to be sitting it out. At Edgbaston, I've bowled really well and felt brilliant before, in the second innings, I experience my side tug as I run into bowl. I tell no one and run back in. At the exact same point of the delivery stride it does so again, only worse. I tell Broady, stationed at mid-on. I say I can bowl on. He gives me a look, the one that only him and Cooky have licence to, and tells me not to. 'You'll make it much worse,' he says, with a logic I don't want to hear but know I need to listen to.

The pitch is green – sickeningly green. I would have loved bowling on it. It does something horrible to me to miss out on cricket now – like every time my body pulls up, I feel the volume of the doubters – of the people waiting for my career to end – turned up. It causes me to question my own sanity.

The conditions are perfect for Broady. Chris Rogers: perfect line and length, caught Cooky. Smith: squared up in the same over, caught Root. Shaun Marsh: caught driving by Ian Bell. 15/4. Adam Voges: huge outside edge, Ben Stokes, diving full length to his right, plucking it out of the air in a moment of magic. 21/5. Broad is running towards Stokes, his hands over his mouth, eyes as wide as they will go. Michael Clarke: well taken by Alastair Cook. A five-wicket haul in 19 balls.

As all the wickets fall, I am caught up in the drama of it all, the sheer chaos that he has created in one morning's cricket. I am always in awe of his ability to bowl spells like this. It's as if he can create something on cue, just as and when the team need it. He creates theatre with either his reaction to the ball he has just bowled, a word with the batter or revving up the crowd. Then, it is as if his knees pump higher, where he turns a game on its head almost just by identifying the moment he wants to. It's an unusual, precious skill. Nobody can get the ball out of his hand at times like these. On this afternoon, Broad takes 8–15, Australia being bowled out for 60 before we regain the Ashes. I forget myself and my own sadness at not being there, jumping up with every wicket on the balcony, as one of the crowd. My only regret as Broady leaves the field is not that I'm injured, but that I haven't been able to watch him do it all from mid-off, as usual.

CHAPTER 44

LIFE IN ONE DAY

It's a phone call. A short one. Andrew Strauss is the director of cricket now and he has some news to deliver to me. England are no longer going to consider me for selection for one-day cricket. They are going to move on and look for other bowlers while allowing me to play Test cricket. I do not understand the decision, nor the reasoning behind it. I am the all-time highest wicket taker in England's white ball history. I am still bowling well. There is still so much to do, so much more to achieve. Does he think I'm reaching the end of my career, at 33? He must do, because he's putting an end to one side of it. I feel from his tone that he is suggesting maybe trying to get another couple of years out of my Test career.

History and experience will tell you this is rational and realistic planning, but I know, in my body, that I am nowhere near the end. The response that comes from within is instinctive and survivalistic. I have reached the place I have against many odds. It goes against every choice I have made in my life up until this point to accept that I should stand down. The way the game has taught me to evolve, to keep fighting, searching for those deep reserves, each time finding I can go further than I'd imagined.

I don't know then that this will be a blessing, nor can I accept his quite logical reasoning that it will help prolong my Test career by managing my workloads, nor does it soften the blow that he is doing the same thing to Broady. Since the Flower team that went to Bavaria and beyond, there are only three remaining; myself, Broad and Cook. We have developed a closeness, in part due to the sheer shared experience, and a tendency to diffuse the pressure with play, bonding us together with an understanding that is unexplainable to anyone outside. We have become close friends – in touch through the days, communicating on not just cricket and regularly spending time at each other's houses. I no longer think of them as teammates, but as close friends. It makes sense that us three will take the long form team forward together and focus on that while the short form side goes in another direction. But a part of me is activated that will not accept any of the reasons. Instead, I can only say the same thing my body does – that I can still do this. I listen to my body and it gives me nothing but the desire to keep going. I refuse to retire officially from one-day cricket. I decide not to announce anything. I know the likelihood now of a return to the format is incredibly slim, given the tone with which this has been delivered to me, but I refuse to turn my back on it, even if it turns its back on me. If they need me, I will still be ready to do a job.

When the news breaks, I am honest with anyone that asks. I don't think it's correct, I think I have more to give, but I respect the decision if they truly think it's in their best interests. As I do so, the question creeps into my existence, at first weekly with a general out-of-interest air to it, but then it morphs into a daily, constant and borderline intrusive one: when do you think you will retire?

I go to see Mark Bawden – no longer working for the team – to talk to him about it. We go to the pub together, finding a table out of the way. I tell him that every five minutes, people are asking me when I'm going to retire. I feel nothing in my body or my performances that suggests I should even be entertaining it. He listens, sympathetically. Together, over one pub lunch, we concoct an approach. Every time I am asked it, or I hear it being talked about, rather than turning it into an emotional thing, why don't I reverse it and use it as singular motivation? I like proving people wrong, he says, and this is a golden opportunity to do exactly that. I thrive off confounding expectations, he says; think of it that way.

As the Strauss verdict lands and I get back to playing, I realise reluctantly that it's probably a good thing. I start to turn my ambitions to playing Test cricket for as long as I can. If I keep working hard, doing the horrible stuff daily in the gym, pushing through every morning that I wake up feeling like I don't want to run, every evening that I go to sleep not being able to brush my teeth, or unable to sit down because of a workload throughout the day, I can get through it; I can go further. I start to see it as an exciting challenge – to get to my forties still playing at the highest level. It would feel like breaking new ground.

Ryan Giggs and Tom Brady are sportspeople in other disciplines who push me towards it, showing me what's possible. British runner Jo Pavey, too, had a second child at 40 and still competed in the Commonwealth Games. If she could do that, I could keep going. Some people think age determines how we behave and what we can do. I start to realise that it isn't the case and, as I watch teammates every year retire through injury or lack of form, I begin to treat it like a duty to myself, of a commitment back to cricket too, to not think about the end of my career from a legacy perspective or as something to get through, but to keep going, keep pushing, keep playing, keep hold of the thing I had dreamed up and miraculously came true, until either I couldn't get on the field or it would turn its back on me.

In the off season, before a series begins, I take on more training than I have ever done. The work happens before the cricket even comes into view. I do weights in the gym on Monday, Wednesday and Friday. I work on my arms, legs and core. It's tough, repetitive and arduous work, where I have to remind myself every morning that wickets are on the other side of it, somewhere down the line. On Tuesday, Thursday and Saturday I am doing a mixture of shuttle sprints, between 40, 50 and 60 metres. Then some longer distance running between 3 and 7 km. In between all of that is interval training, either four minutes running and two minutes off or two minutes on and one minute off or one minute on, one minute off, all done on the running track. I swim a couple of times a week. I load all this into my body daily, thinking about the cricket simultaneously, visualising who I will be bowling at and how I will get them out so that when it comes around, I just have to unlock what is already inside.

CHAPTER 45

STILL JIMMY

19–21 May 2016

ENGLAND vs SRI LANKA, 1st Test, *Headingley, Leeds*

England 298; Sri Lanka 91 and 119

England won by an innings and 88 runs

Sri Lanka 1st innings: **J Anderson 11.4–6–16–5**; 2nd innings:
J Anderson 13.3–5–29–5

Although every summer now rolls into the next, a routine of cricket, then family, then cricket, then family, forming my life's structure, I am entering a phase of consistency with the ball that I have not yet reached. As I do so, the voices outside grow louder on the subject of retirement. It starts or ends every conversation. The better I play, the more it is talked about. It is like fighting against the elements, walking against that current back in Burnley, up that hill, on to that bench where I can be whoever I want to be.

Despite the outside chaos, I am feeling more and more in

control. I know that I can block outside thoughts. That is all they are, thoughts. I am in control of how everything moves. My mindset during games now moves less frequently to the wilder emotions and the sulks. When I find myself there, I speak to myself quickly, reset and begin again. I am also taking myself outside of cricket more regularly, to keep my body at the absolute height of its performance. I am focusing much more on the technique of running itself. Without a ball in hand I do hip drills daily, take to hurdle sprint work and spend lots of time watching sprinters take off out of the markers, their economy of movement and efficiency through the air, as I try to get myself somewhere close to what they do when I run up. I am running faster than I have in years, my body feeding off its input and adapting into an evolved state of athleticism I have never reached before.

Maybe most importantly, I am also finding that cricket keeps asking new questions, presenting new challenges, and in turn, now that the self-doubt and self-worth paranoia that plagued me in the early part of my career are quietened, I am beginning to just enjoy it. We are at Headingley for the Sri Lanka series that forms half of the summer. When we get there, Broady and I have the sudden realisation that we both always bowl from the same end and both of us struggle. I would usually run downhill and Broady would start up the hill at the Football Ground End. It's never really worked. We shrug at each other before play – is it worth swapping ends?

Jonny Bairstow has batted brilliantly on a difficult pitch, puffing his chest out in his trademark way and putting the bad balls away. I've watched and waited, trying to calculate what the difference will be from the other end. Up the hill, running in, it encourages me to run faster, to surge myself against the current. Where the opposite end at Headingley can con you into bowling too full, it's the opposite up the hill. It's a battle against bowling slightly too short. The ball feels like it kicks off the surface more though and I enjoy all the opposing causes and effects it creates.

To Kaushal Silva, I get the ball to kick from just back of a length. He edges behind to Bairstow. Then I'm pushing the ball into Angelo Mathews' pads, angling in, trapping him LBW. It's all about patiently probing a similar line, little variations, not allowing them any respite whatsoever. To Dasun Shanaka, I get the ball to shape away from the right-hander, leaving him with the ball hanging. Then Rangana Herath, the same to a left-hander. Finally, Shaminda Eranga, a reviewed caught behind. They are all out for 91 and I have a five-for to my name. Cooky asks if I feel like I can bowl again, putting them in to follow on. He doesn't even need an answer. Not even a day later, I have another five wickets, steering England to an innings victory. I've never felt stronger, running up the hill, running so hard it almost feels like I'm running away from something – maybe all the retirement questions, still against the tide, still walking out of somewhere, still getting to some place new, still plenty of cricket to play, no matter what they all say.

A year later, I'll take my 500th wicket for England at 35 years old, before a week later recording career best innings figures of 7–42 against the West Indies, now with Joe Root as the captain. It's all continual, uphill momentum. Anyone who said I couldn't go on was just another voice to prove wrong.

CHAPTER 46

TAILENDERS

Before we leave for the Ashes tour of 2017–18, I get a call from Greg James, the presenter of BBC Radio 1's flagship breakfast show, asking if I'd like to do a new podcast with him called *Tailenders* for the BBC. I'd really enjoyed working with Greg and producer Mark 'Sharky' Sharman on a show we had done previously alongside Swanny called *Not Just Cricket*, so I say, of course. He says he's got Felix White from the band The Maccabees involved, a band that Swanny and I had raced from an abandoned South Africa one-day game to go and see at Reading Festival a few years earlier. The Maccabees have just split and Felix loves cricket, and Greg thinks it will work. Sounds good, I say, expecting us to do a few episodes while I'm in Australia.

A few episodes in, I'm taken by surprise by how much I'm enjoying it. Speaking to people who have seen me play from the outside and are so clearly passionate about the game helps me to see my career through a new lens. At first, I'm amazed the episodes come out so well and are so warmly received. To me, they seem like general rambling chats that I assume are barely serviceable as a BBC podcast, but it appears our style of casually presenting cricket from every aspect has connected with people very quickly. Callers get in touch with the show every week, spinning us into conversations away from the current Ashes series that's in progress and more towards how cricket lives in the imagination. These conversations open something up in myself. I end up realising that cricket has infiltrated my system so much that when I walk over a pavement slab, and my foot is over the crack, I'll think to myself, *Shit, no ball*. People phone in to tell us about playing all kinds of different cricket in their sixties or even older too. It begins to inspire me again to notice that cricket is such a portal for communication and release, and in turn the fun and enjoyment sends me back into the game with a refreshed view on it.

In our third episode, a Bristolian called Matt Horan phones in. He invented a roll-up vending machine shoe company called Rollasole, he explains. He doesn't have any interest in cricket, having just heard of the show as a Maccabees fan, but thinks he has a cricketing familial tie we might be interested in. He is distantly related to, he claims, Sachin Tendulkar. As we try to explain that Tendulkar might be the greatest cricketer who ever lived, the show then trips itself into a left-field, on the fly comedy exploring whether Matt is indeed related to Sachin Tendulkar. We lovingly call him Mattchin Tendulkar, and within a few episodes, he's a cricketing cult hero. He's not just a roll-up shoe salesman, it turns out, but with every passing week has more and more questions about cricket and ideas about how it might be made more interesting to the wider public. The four of us and Sharky begin a friendship, playing out in recorded episodes every week that accidentally explain cricket from every side – from total beginner to musician to broadcaster to cricketer – and before we know it, we will be recording every week together for the next seven years.

Some years later, Mattchin will pose an absurd theoretical question to me, asking if a wizard came up to me and offered me another ten years of my career, but the cost was I would always have a frog chasing me that would kill me if I touched it, would I take it? It prompts people to turn up to Tests wearing wizard and frog costumes, pretending to chase me around. People shout 'go well' at me, a *Tailenders* code for being a listener, to which you have to reply 'cheers', as a nod to the stereotypical sports interview ending. And every week, listeners around the world share their deepest cricket humiliations, hoping to be alleviated of their pain by having me read it out as Felix plays sad guitar music behind it. Before we know it, we are going on tour, with live bands, playing the London Palladium and the Apollo, and I'm dressing up as alter ego 'Timmy Banderson', who plays short-form franchise cricket and is under no scrutiny about when he might retire. For some reason Timmy is American too and skateboards on to the stage.

From time to time, my teammates come on the show. When they do, they stare at me, quite confused by what they see, as if they're watching someone completely different. For all of us, it doesn't consciously land, but it's a form of play and connection, a release from our everyday lives, and through it, it helps breed a new exuberance and a sense of youth and novelty to a game I have been entrenched in for decades.

We are beaten soundly in Australia and as Geoffrey Boycott

quizzes me after the last game, asking who's going to be responsible for this defeat, I tell him that it might be a question for someone above my pay grade and that I very much doubt I will be coming back to Australia as a 39-year-old, so maybe they should look to the future there. Everyone laughs. Even the idea of doing that, as a fast bowler, is laughable.

CHAPTER 47

KOHLI AND COOK

1–4 August 2018

ENGLAND vs INDIA, 1st Test, *Edgbaston, Birmingham*

England 287 and 180; India 274 and 162

England won by 31 runs

India 1st innings: V Kohli 149

7–11 September 2018

ENGLAND vs INDIA, 5th Test, *The Oval, London*

England 332 and 423/8 dec.; India 292 and 345

England won by 118 runs

England 2nd innings: A Cook 147; India 2nd innings:
J Anderson 22.3–11–45–3

Ever since he has been touted as the next Tendulkar, Virat Kohli has been someone on my radar. It is something that has become a pattern of my relationship with the external world – these rivalries and battles with other key players from India, Australia and beyond. As the leader of the England attack, my thoughts are always on the talismanic batter for the other team. Both of us set the tone and some of the character of our sides.

Kohli has come to England in 2018 with a reputation for being the best in the world – a generational talent at his peak. I had the better of him in the last series in England in 2014, and he's come back now with a desire to prove he can do it outside of his most natural conditions. I understand this aspiration to push yourself to the outer reaches of your ability, to be fuelled by something within that keeps you going. India arrive with realistic intentions of winning in England for the first time in many years and, as our orbits circle each other, there are moments before the series where our paths cross.

I am with Felix and Greg recording a *Tailenders* episode on the outfield at Lord's and we walk past him. On meeting Kohli's eyes, the other Tailenders pause to acknowledge the change in my tone – the way we unflinchingly look at each other, like boxers before a fight, our first blows thrown before we even get in the ring.

It's the first Test at Edgbaston and I am at the top of my mark, our eyes meeting again as he turns to face the next ball. I know that the ball is moving and just as I had found that extra level when first bowling to Kohli's predecessor, Tendulkar, all those years ago, I breathe at my mark, feel the seam on my fingers and run in to bowl. There is a heightened concentration and intensity today, as if me vs Kohli is not just a part of England vs India, but a separate battle in its own universe.

I am getting the ball to swing at ease, teasing him with deliveries outside his off stump. He is determined to leave the ball there, fighting within himself to not do what he did last tour and leave his bat hanging outside the off stump and edge behind. A few whistle past the off stump. I try to drag him across the stumps, every ball landing exactly where I want it to, before the odd one very rarely just comes into his pads. One falls just short of the diving hands of Jos Buttler at fourth slip. He edges another but does so with soft hands, falling just short of Jonny Bairstow. He's not scoring any runs – but runs are not on the agenda. It's about his survival and my hunting. That is the battle. He edges again, falling just short of Keaton Jennings.

Every ball is met with a silence beforehand and then followed by a sigh or a gasp from the slip cordon as Kohli hangs on. The exact sequence plays out over after over, tiny variations on a theme, both of our temperaments and discipline being tested. I finally get a genuine edge and as I go up to celebrate, Jennings dives in front of Dawid Malan at second slip, blinding his view for a second, and the ball spills out of Malan's hands. It's a reprieve. Kohli has survived. He goes on to score 149, his first century in England, expanding after getting through the initial arm wrestle between us. It's one of the times I don't get the better of him in England, but the other side of this fight is not hurt or self-recrimination, it's a different feeling. For the couple of hours that we dovetailed, locked in a runless battle, we demonstrated something particular about the art of Test cricket with both bat and ball and though he had got through somehow, I felt a kinship and sense of completion with someone from the other side of the world who was also prepared to go to the same lengths and depths for the game.

Two weeks later, immediately after the third Test of the series at Trent Bridge, Alastair Cook asks if he can speak to me.

He has decided to retire at the end of this series, he says. It's taken too much out of him – all the mental challenges of having to live with thinking about Test cricket off the pitch, the time he has to put into captaincy, the out-of-form periods that come with constant scrutiny and critique, the energy that the game has required – it all feels like he's lost that tiny edge that is required and he wants to go on his own terms. He says that he's telling me first because I'm his best friend in the team and he wants to see how it feels coming out of his mouth. It feels right, he says. It's been 12 years since that plane journey when we first sat next to each other and he uttered the immortal words, 'The last time we met, you called me a c**t.' I don't think either of us would have believed we would have been on the balcony of Trent Bridge 12 years later, as best mates and the senior members of the England Test team for some time, sharing this moment. He will announce it before the last Test but until then, we keep it to ourselves.

In Alastair Cook's last ever innings for England, he scores a hundred at The Oval. Cricket fans from inside South London and beyond watch on, awestruck and emotional, wider memories of the time spent and all of the lives lived watching Cooky make cricket work for him. I feel like for all the time we have spent together, all the hours upon hours he has stacked up, maybe I've watched him the least. Just like at Brisbane in 2010/11, when we were both top of the world in our respective disciplines, I fall asleep during his innings. Some would say it was a damning appraisal of his batting that I would rather be in the back of the dressing room fast asleep than watching it. The other way you could look at it is that it was all safe when he was batting. There was no alarm. Sleeping was a safe bet. I am not woken by any of the applause that wraps itself around The Oval for minutes as he brings up his hundred, the only person in England sleeping through it.

The final day of the last Test is tense and India are chasing a reachable target. As darkness threatens to descend on South London, we finally run through their batters in the afternoon but they still have time to hold on to draw. Joe Root asks for a new ball and hands it to me. Mohammed Shami is batting. Cooky is at slip, his last moments as a Test cricketer dimming with the light. I run in and get the ball to move into him, missing his defensive stroke, his middle stump flying. It's my 564th Test wicket and with it I go past Glenn McGrath's total on the all-time list. Cooky runs up to me, his broad grin shining in my face, and hugs me, as if a huge torment has been lifted off him, and we walk off side by side, in conversation, just like that first flight. We have won 4-1.

I conduct the interview straight after with my first ever wicket, Ian Ward, who stands in front of me, microphone in hand as tears swell. 'You're going to miss him, aren't you?' he says. I feel the confusing mixture of exhaustion and emotion as I try to laugh off the tears. 'Absolutely, yeah,' I say, feeling the 12 years throw themselves into my chest. 'He's my best mate and ...' I can't get the words out any more, pure emotion and heartbreak and gratitude finding their way out to penetrate through any sense of a normal post-match interview. 'He's been brilliant.' Every word feels like it takes an army to get out. 'Just to always be there for me.'

When alcohol has dulled our senses and eased the flow of words, Cooky is standing next to me in front of an emptied Oval. It's the last time we will be together with a series won, the ghosts of everything that has happened still inside the ground, and just the two of us understanding what we have been through. 'I think he's England's greatest ever cricketer,' Cooky says about me, deflecting from it all being about him. 'How many wickets has it been now, 564?' They both turn to me. I shrug: 'I've lost count.'

Kohli isn't one of them this year, but I can live with that.

CHAPTER 48

INJURED ASHES

1 August –16 September 2019

It's the evening of Cooky's final Test and I'm waking up to find an empty dressing room: family, friends and players gone. I have missed the celebrations again – all the physical exertion and emotional exhaustion, my mind wanting nothing but a deep sleep. I come to, curled up on the corner of the bench in the dressing room at The Oval, whites still on, cap and jumper splayed out across the floor, my gear still everywhere but everyone else is gone. It's like I'm the last man to ever be in the England team. A vision comes to me of holding on to being an England player even when all the cricket is gone, still there saying, 'No, I'm not done yet, this isn't over.' I test out the words Cooky said to me at Trent Bridge. How would they feel coming out of my mouth? There is no part of them that fits, not one of them that feels like they are my own. I am not thinking about any particular legacy moment or number of wickets to hit. I am put on earth to do this, to see the ball do what it does and to turn batters into S shapes. I will play on.

It's 2019 and I am desperate to have a good Ashes – unperturbed by a Trevor Bayliss team talk in which he says, 'I've got just one word today I want you all to remember', before pausing, scratching his head and saying, 'I've forgotten what it is now.' I manage only four overs in the first Ashes Test at Edgbaston though before a calf injury rules me out. I try to bat the next innings to help the team but end up damaging it more while taking off for a run. I will play no further part than half a morning's cricket in the entire series. The media and papers are awash with it being the end of my career – that there is every chance I will never play for England again. I get home, limp through the door, and choose to go as far away from cricket as I can.

We are in Greece when the Ashes unfolds as Jofra Archer lands a bouncer on Steve Smith's head at Lord's, leaving him splayed out on the floor. Then I'm in the dressing room, watching in awe along with everyone else as Ben Stokes plays maybe the greatest innings of all time to win the Headingley Test. He had done the same thing earlier in the year – alongside Jos Buttler – to win the World Cup for the first time for England. It's an odd sensation to be both on the outside and the inside during these moments, still the leader of the attack in theory, but injured and out of view as cricket comes back into focus again. It's like the Ashes of 2005 and the stress fracture the year that followed repeating themselves all over again. There is no doubt in my mind, nothing that tells me I've had enough. I will get myself fit, work harder than ever before and as if nothing has happened before and those 564 wickets are now wiped clean, prove I'm all the bowlers I've ever been. No outside definition of the boundaries of age will stop me.

CHAPTER 49

LOCKDOWN

I have spent lockdown – like anyone else – worrying, walking around the house, wondering what to do. *Tailenders* comes into its own as we do quizzes and regularly meet up on zoom, it becoming its own universe of something to look forward to. We start a little charity – the Go Well Fund – to help with causes affected by Covid. At some point during the lockdown, as *Tailenders* rolls out from weekly episodes to constant communication with each other, I find myself watching the India vs Australia series late into the night, rolling my eyes while the rest of them make wild and inaccurate observations on almost every single aspect and session of the game. We begin to realise during lockdown that cricket – from each of our different perspectives – has meant so much to us. It's been a constant excuse for communication, for distraction when required, and for explaining our own lives to others when we needed it.

As we roll out shows twice a week, it becomes clear that many people across the country, or even the world, feel the same thing. It's becoming symbolic for the condition of the world to move through a summer where pitches are vacated and nets are unused. It also lands in a more meaningful way to me as it asks me: what has it meant to play cricket for England for so long? I begin to meditate on the privilege of being a vessel for which people channel their lives through, especially as time extends and my life becomes measurable through theirs. I hadn't stopped to think that babies might be born and loved ones lost with Test cricket as the backdrop or that whatever I've been doing inside a ground might also be reverberating outside in a lasting way.

As we use the time to reflect on what cricket has meant to all of us, and what we are going to use it for when (if) the world comes back, we build plans for a score-along. Calls are had and exceptions made and we, collaboratively with Sky, arrange for them to play back the entirety of the last day of Ben Stokes's Headingley innings against Australia. The idea is that we can relive it exactly as it went down, remembering how Test cricket used to hum around in the background of your day-to-day. In my case, it's the foreground, but it's interesting to view it with a fresh perspective and to start to realise how Test cricket works with people's imaginations – informing and feeding and offering escape for all who love it.

Before the score-along, we release a single on vinyl. I have designed the album artwork on my phone – a vague nod to The Maccabees' first single – with our illustrated heads dotting up in a row across the cover. Inside it, Mattchin does a spoken word poem about his Christmas single over some music Felix has made for *The Edge* film, and for the B-side, which we record a tender, passionate ode to Sharky's favourite cricketer: 'Allan Lamb', live on the podcast. We don't get the logistics in order in time, so the

Christmas single comes out in March. It turns out that it's quite a genius piece of accidental marketing and charts at number five in the UK physical charts. It has words and the chords are not dissimilar to 'Everybody Hurts' by R.E.M. We are not thinking too much about any of it, but somehow the show has its own feeling and connection, and we come to realise that what we are recording is a group of people genuinely becoming good friends, no real overthought to it, just a strange coincidence of lives turning an idea into a source of comfort that means so much to those who are listening to it.

After the score-along, we decide that Mattchin will host a quiz. He is fast becoming a cricketing cult hero, phoning into the show every week with more 'ideas' on how to make Test cricket more accessible or with quizzes – almost always entirely lifted from another TV gameshow, then renamed and loosely made about cricket. We encourage all of it even if I, knowingly, shrug and shun my way through his insistence on telling people that not only is Sachin Tendulkar his uncle, but Jimmy Anderson is his best friend too.

It is agreed that for the quiz, Mattchin should have access to my Instagram account as it has 1 million followers and because that way we can get the most 'eyeballs' on the quiz. I'm a bit dubious about it, but dutifully hand over the password and tell Mattchin to give it a go. I'm braced in trepidation during the score-along about how this will go down. Meanwhile, Tailenders all over the country score the game, sending us in their scorecards, some of them so detailed and precise, using colour pens and everything, that they look like artworks fitting of the day itself. It also occurs to us while watching that the day itself is a strange kind of metaphor for what we are doing in lockdown – a group of people, from the team to the crowd, willing something true, staying in the moment and making something happen through sheer love and will. The commentary too only flickering my conscience for the first time.

When the quiz comes around, I am logging in from the *Tailenders* account. Mattchin has clearly put in a lot of effort and as soon as he logs on, on my account, 3,000 people are on immediately, causing the app to be in trouble. Mattchin has been preparing all week. He has researched all the guests that are coming on – teammate and fast becoming a national hero Mark Wood, chef Ainsley Harriott, musician Nadine Shah, TV presenter Gregg Wallace, musician Ed O'Brien from Radiohead and broadcaster Isa Guha. Mattchin is over-psyched, put out by the amount of quizzes that are suddenly being done through lockdown, desperate to put his marker down. When people enter the quiz, there is a holding slide in Mattchin's front room. The holding slide alerts people to the fact that Jimmy's Instagram has not been hacked and that he's hosting a quiz with my permission. It's well thought through. What isn't that well thought through is the fact that the sign is the wrong way round, the camera reversing the image to mean everything is back to front to what he thinks it is. Selfie mode mirrors the text, it turns out. It looks like I've logged on to my Instagram live, 'Soul Limbo' playing in the background, with a text resembling Chinese on the sign.

I log into Mattchin's account and we have the first round of the quiz. It goes relatively smoothly, setting up the quiz and the premise. Then Greg joins Mattchin, inexplicably in a wide-brimmed hat, and gets through a round of questions. The problem is, Mattchin doesn't have an incredible grasp of Instagram and then tries to let his next guest in, Isa Guha. The phone isn't complying. Every time he tries to let her in, his camera is spun around to show his hallway. He starts making panicked sounds, telling himself everything is OK. His hallway appears again and again. Someone comments, 'I've seen Mattchin's light switch more than I've seen Jimmy Anderson.' The live comments are coming in. There's a lot of confusion and instructions from the listeners. He keeps trying different buttons. None of them work. 'Right, I can't,' he says as he starts to get angry in his tuxedo, pulling his bow tie loose. 'Look, too many people are trying to sign in.'

I am watching this play out, my head in my hands, a disaster unfolding on my Instagram page, everything going down in my name. Mattchin decides – after showing everyone his hall for the 27th time – that he's going to log off and back on. He announces this to the tens of thousands of people who have tuned in. No one is logging off. The worse this goes, the more people join. When Mattchin comes back on, on my Instagram, my profile photo has gone and there is no sound. Now Mattchin looks very stressed and I am worried about getting a call about fraud soon. Mattchin is going beet red and now Ed O'Brien and Ainsley Harriott are messaging, trying to help him out. As he panics, he frantically presses anything he can on his phone, which then starts to generate the little filters from my daughters that I have saved on my phone. 'What Premier League team am I?' he asks, with a little cartoon bird now suddenly appearing. 'How old do I look?' The more he panics, the more stuff starts appearing on his head. By the time he logs off for a second time, my Instagram profile has been lost. They clearly think someone has stolen my phone and it's been reported multiple times. I've lost a lot of followers and I cannot get in.

When we come back, a message has gone round, to join the quiz on Greg and Mattchin's profiles. Everyone has stayed and found Mattchin's account – they all want to see this car crash prolong. With Greg and Mattchin now on, Mattchin is trying to do a pre-prepared, Royal Variety Performance that brings Mark Wood in. Mark's quiz is called 'Mark Your Cards'. The idea is that Greg will say stop while he is dealing the pack and the card will have 'Mark Wood' written on it, which will in turn introduce to the quiz, Mark Wood. Mattchin has forgotten that the screen is reversing everything though, and when he tries to do this, he proudly and manically shows the card upside down. The word Mark Wood, it turns out, when reversed and then held upside down, seems to say 'Mood Wank'.

Wood, who has given up on the quiz by now and left, messages me half an hour later asking why he's getting thousands of messages that say 'mood wank'. It's hard to explain. The only thing I say is that, if it's any consolation, the phrase is trending on Twitter, sitting at number two behind 'coronavirusnews'. The only person who is disappointed is my dad, who has been watching the entire thing unfold and messages me saying, 'I was six out of six there. What happened to the rest of the questions?' It takes weeks to get my Instagram account verified again.

CHAPTER 50

600

21–25 August 2020

ENGLAND vs PAKISTAN, 3rd Test, Rose Bowl, Southampton

England 583/8 dec.; Pakistan 273 and 187/4 (following on)

Match drawn

England 1st innings: **Z Crawley 267** and **J Buttler 152**

Pakistan 1st innings: **A Ali 141 n.o.**

Pakistan 2nd innings: **A Ali c Root b Anderson 31** (600th Test wicket)

The country is locked down and cricket dissolves into the air as if it is from a hazy past life. We are delighted when Pakistan and West Indies agree to come to England to tour. Most of the UK, and the rest of the world for that matter, is in isolation, all in varying degrees of boredom or distress, yet we are going to be allowed to play. It becomes almost like some small version of National Service, to give people something to watch that is happening out in the world and try to impart a feeling of normality into their lives. The protocols are tight and intense. We are tested multiple times daily, masks are required to always be worn when we're indoors and we must always stay at the grounds we are playing at, never being allowed out of the rooms. We eat individually, with screens separating each of us. The only saving grace is that the rooms often have balconies, meaning we can pop our heads out and sit there, talking, as if we're cellmates trying to squeeze our heads through bars, hatching our plans to escape.

It's the last Test before everyone can finally get home to see their families. The isolation and the eerie repetition of completely empty grounds has given the series an apocalyptic feel, even if it's a lifeline to cricket fans on the outside. It sometimes feels like the world has ended and against all the odds, the only thing to survive has been Test cricket, stubbornly forcing its way on, batters playing and leaving to deserted landscapes while I huff, puff and force myself to carry on bowling the channels required. Maybe this is what cricket has always felt like to me. If this is the only thing left to do in the world, I will be happy doing it forever, regardless of what is happening on the outside.

We've all grown longer hair and beards and with the endless isolation, nerves are more frayed. I am chasing my 600th wicket for England. I keep saying that it doesn't matter, that it will be the same as any other wicket, but it is not. It is gnawing away at me. I keep reading and hearing that no seamer has ever taken 600 wickets in the history of cricket. Every time I do, a part of me worries that it is jinxed and that I'll forever be frozen on 599, bowling to no one, hair and beard growing longer, sky growing darker, winter intruding into my space. As I do, my emotionless side that I worked on with Bawden vanishes. This is no time for the emotionless.

My teammates are not helping with this. On day four, they keep dropping catches, like they are in on the conspiracy to leave me stuck on 599. They drop four catches in 37 balls, each of them leaving me more and more angry. Finally, the ball is teed up gently to Stuart Broad at mid-on. It is passively in the air for long enough to leave me a moment to sigh inwardly, that the wicket is finally taken, and we can all move on. Broad goes to take it to his side, the easiest catch anyone will take at any level, and it somehow bounces out, cannoning off his side and on to the floor. He picks up the ball out of sheer anger and hurls it at the stumps as they attempt a shell-shocked run. Mohammad Abbas has been caught up in the moment himself and is way out of his ground. It hits middle stump. Not one England player celebrates, all of them instead sheepishly walking towards me and Stuart, like schoolchildren who know how much trouble they are in. When they get to me, Jos Buttler is covering his smile with his wicketkeeper glove, almost giggling in nervous response. I will find it funny one day, but not now.

A day later, the game is petering out into a draw because of the rain. I am bowling, still searching for the wicket. Everyone dutifully goes about their business, knowing their isolation is almost over and the game certainly a dead rubber. Stuart Broad is stationed at mid-on, hands on hips. I ask him what he thinks I should bowl. Normally, he's good with this, full of ideas, giving me things to think about. This time, he shrugs. I have never seen him shrug like that in the field. I ask him what's wrong. 'We shouldn't be playing, it's too wet,' he says. 'The only reason we're here is because of you.'

As he says it, I remember the last Ashes series in Australia, the one where we had been destroyed 4-0. I had been given out in the last rites, caught behind, the game won by a distance by Australia, everyone just relieved to finish and go home. I didn't think I'd hit it. 'I've not hit it,' I'm telling everyone. 'It isn't out,' as they roll their eyes and clear up the stumps. In my mind then, I only needed a career-best triple century to win a consolation game for England. You just never know.

In the same spell that Broady has shrugged at me, I get a ball to bounce slightly more sharply than a few of the previous deliveries and find Azhar Ali's outside edge. Joe Root takes the catch and as everyone swamps me, relieved and half-apologetic, all wanting to go home, I take the ball and, tongue in cheek, raise it to each corner of the completely empty ground.

I have to do media interviews as the game is finally called a draw, spending 45 minutes on the outfield being interviewed by journalists at a long distance, all of them asking whether this means retirement is any closer. I say no to each of them, that it doesn't mean anything and that I will keep playing for as long as my body lets me. They all nod back, half-believing yet slightly bemused. I get back to the dressing room and discover that every single person has left. It's like there's a theme developing here, me being left alone in these empty dressing rooms. We'll have to celebrate another time then, I think to myself, and pack up to get home to see the girls.

CHAPTER 51

COVID

8 December 2021 – 18 January 2022

AUSTRALIA vs ENGLAND, five Test matches

Australia won the series 4-0

We're flying out to Australia in a week. I'm dreading this Ashes. I don't know anyone who isn't. Covid protocol is extremely tight still and the world is still in and out of lockdown. We've been given information about what the tour will be like – that there will be severe restrictions compared to what we're used to. It's my mum's 60th and we're at an Airbnb in the Lake District. If the family stay as a bubble and don't go out anywhere, we think, it should be fine. We get tested at home. They come to our house, masked and gloved, and one by one move through the family, poking the swab as far as it will go up each nostril. We are all clear, they tell us.

In the Lake District, we go and meet my mum and dad, sister and brother-in-law too. We are having a lovely evening, watching *Strictly*, doing the most ordinary things that have now become rare and sacred. The tour will be so isolated, so lonely, so horrible, that I am just taking it in while I can, a level of neutrality and ease. It is imminent too as I'm leaving in a week. The next day, as we are walking, I get a phone call: Lola has tested positive for Covid. I'm suddenly struck cold. I shouldn't be here. In a panic, no physical contact, a flash of rushed goodbyes, we are packing up. 'We shouldn't really be here,' I am suddenly saying to them. 'We have to go.' We drive home together, the windows wide open, everyone facing forward in masks, as if a nuclear disaster is upon us.

As soon as I get home, the England medical team tell me that I can't be at home any more. If there's any chance of me going on tour, I have to leave immediately, with no more physical contact with anyone. I'm packing my bags in silence, suddenly ruptured from my family. I'm just going to leave quietly, not make this any worse than it needs to be. We all know that, best case scenario, I will not be back for three months now. That's going to be extended by an extra week, where I get an Airbnb on Altrincham High Street, in a small upstairs flat. I'm told, in very strict detail, not to leave the flat until I head off for the tour. I spend a week there, just watching the traffic go up and down the same high street, too disconnected from anyone, too cautious to even message and say what has happened. The only company I have is a masked visitor who comes to give me Covid tests every day and then leaves. I am negative. I can travel. But even when I do, I cannot sit with the squad. I need to be waiting in my own room, then on my own at the back of the plane for the duration of the 24 hours to Australia in complete isolation.

I test negative in Queensland but before I am able to rejoin the group, see anyone or get outside, we are all taken to quarantine for two weeks. Inside a single, windowless room, I wait. There is no exercise, no cricket, just my own time and space. By the time we start playing cricket, I have been completely alone for five weeks. The motel in Brisbane, for the first Test, is extremely isolated. There is a very highly monitored space and very little time allowed for preparation. On arrival, they have left each room big boxes as sort of isolation survival packs. They are full of biscuits and chocolates. Imagine the worst possible thing to put in your system before doing high-pressure, athletic sport. It's like Cricket Australia are trying to fatten us up with snack boxes.

The days unwind in endless cycles of *Call of Duty* and Netflix. We are let out for a couple of hours a day to practise, with limited contact. We are not allowed out for dinner, the hotel provide it laid out like a self-service buffet. When food needs to be refilled, everyone must leave the room, pull the shutters down and then wait for it to be announced on the tannoy that we can come back in. It is part prison, part *Black Mirror*, but inside an Ashes tour. It feels like it rains the entire tour.

In preparation for the first game, we cannot bowl because it is too wet. There are no indoor nets. To get miles in our legs, Phil Scott, the strength and conditioning coach, lays out treasure hunts for us around Brisbane. We are sent off individually on these hunts to find monuments. Even before the first ball, we are weathered and beaten, putting on brave faces as best we can, as the encircling media from home and Australia stretch themselves to judge us. Rory Burns is bowled first ball, one around his legs. It's a dismissal that is months in the making – a fate already decided by the preparation, and one that will play out across an entire, miserable tour around Australia.

The daily Covid tests are so brutal that you feel like they are almost intentionally trying to reach your brain through your nose. On Christmas Day, we are sent to the beach and they give us hot dogs on white bread. It's starting to feel like such a prisoner captive situation that you daren't even ask for ketchup. If any players get Covid, there are full hazmat suits for anyone who has been around them. By the end of the tour, the word survival is being used regularly but never in a cricket sense. Everyone is desperate to go home, and it shows.

The madness begins to extend into a paranoia and slightly edgy thinking between all of us. I really like Chris Silverwood but the alien intensity of the situation has understandably taken its toll. Rory Burns is dropped at Melbourne and he finds out through the media. Burns is upset that he hasn't heard from anyone inside the camp. Silverwood is livid about the leak and hears that it has come through Broady's ghost writer for his column. Silverwood pulls Broady in, volleying him with a tirade about the leak. Broad doesn't know anything about the leak and pleads his innocence. A few days later, it turns out that the leak has come from Silverwood himself, mentioning the team in earshot of the press. He is his own leak. It is that sort of tour. At the start of the same Test, Silverwood and Root have spent half an hour at the pitch on the morning, analysing it. Shane Warne, on television duties, walked past and, taking one glance at it, said, 'What are you looking for, boys? It's clearly a bowl first.' Our heads were all scrambled. It was no one's fault. We had done pretty well just to stay on the tour at all. All the results feel foregone conclusions, and no cricket is even going to be really remembered by anyone who played it. When I get home, everything feels different, like I'm locked out of my own life and in a space where it will take time to remember what the reason for playing cricket really is.

CHAPTER 52

'I WANT JIMMY BACK'

5–9 February 2021

INDIA vs ENGLAND, 1st Test, MA Chidambaram Stadium, Chennai

England 578 and 178; India 337 and 192

England won by 227 runs

England 1st innings: **J Root 218**; India 2nd innings: **J Anderson** 11–4–17–3

As the world gets back to normal, mine continues the same as always – focusing on what and who is next. Living in stubborn denial of age, pushing my body further, still running in, up hills and out of problems and into battle for England. I've bowled one of my favourite overs in my career, dismissing both Shubman Gill and Ajinkya Rahane in Chennai. They are both excellent at home – beautiful technicians and young masters of their conditions – but the ball reverse-swings almost cartoonishly in India and when it does, there is nothing more fun for me in the world. The ball swings back in late and aggressively to both of them, leaving them frozen in perfect orthodox defensive shots, their stumps out of the ground. It's as good a feeling as there is.

Not long after, Ashley Giles, now a coach at Lancashire, gets in touch and tells me that they'd like to name an end at Old Trafford after me. There is the Brian Statham End, but the other end remains nameless at the ground. With the James Anderson End, I would become maybe the only living cricketer to still be bowling at an end named after them. It feels like a huge deal but, to look back on it, to dwell on it, presents some kind of danger to me. To reflect and bathe in it would maybe mean I am done, when I am not. This sort of danger – between being mythologised yet still wanting to continue my career in the flesh – is made more real when a phone call arrives from Andrew Strauss. It's the one that takes place while the girls are with me in the car. It's short and sharp, Strauss informing me that I will not be going on tour to the West Indies. My response is to just get back in the gym, back to work. I have too much more left to give to be shut out now.

When they lose and Joe Root hands over the captaincy to Ben Stokes, my omission is the first thing he brings up in the meeting with new head of cricket, Rob Key. 'I want Jimmy back,' are his first words, to which Key nods and agrees.

At Edgbaston, after I make my return to the side, I take Virat Kohli's wicket again. As I walk off the pitch, he comes up to me and says that he's enjoyed playing against me and it has been a pleasure doing it one final time. 'Why?' I say, 'Are you retiring?'

CHAPTER 53

JUST DON'T CALL IT BAZBALL

May 2022

The phone rings. It's Brendon McCullum. I've been waiting for this call. By any stretch of the imagination, he is a left-field choice as the new long form coach of England as he has no coaching experience at this level. It is 14 years since I first bowled at him, the summer where indescribable magic flowed through my body and showed me that I might be capable of something more than I thought possible. We are different people now, Brendon with a career of innovative and inspiring aggressive cricket behind him.

He is quick with his words and gets to the point: 'I just want to pick the strongest England team, and you will be in that.' A smile moves across my face, another opportunity of rebirth. 'You are very much in our plans.' I am immediately excited, an energy filling me once again. I suddenly feel set apart from the grizzling, stubborn man I have found myself becoming on the field over the last few years. I have been walking the cricket field like a lone ranger who is paranoid someone is following them, clinging to my bowling spot as if it is constantly trying to be snatched away from me.

The first training sessions under Brendon and Ben are unlike any I've ever been part of for a cricket team. Brendon, referred to as Baz, speaks with immediate clarity about how he wants to play. I am struck by how eloquent he is and how clearly he is speaking from the heart. He is calm, clear and to the point. It's a huge change from Chris Silverwood, who would address the team with pre-prepared notes. It's incredible how quickly a message will land if a coach is looking a player in the eyes rather than at their notes. We are all immediately engaged. He says that he won't hands-on in the nets, but his job is to make us all feel ten feet tall and bulletproof when we walk on to the field. I already feel it just by taking the first practice session.

Baz and Ben are very aligned. They want us to entertain. They want us to be a team that people are excited to come and watch. The style of cricket is simple – find ways of putting the opposition under pressure and, if ever in doubt, take the positive option. There are range-hitting drills and very little scrutinised training. Everyone is left to prepare according to their own needs. They both make clear in their understated and unfussy ways that the mentality of this team is going to be different. We will not be playing for draws and the most aggressive or exciting option is always the best one.

There are no stats or analytics, which create a ceiling for how well players play – there is just a freedom to show the world what you can do. Unusual, instinctive fields will be set, bowlers will be at all times encouraged to take wickets, even if it goes for runs. It goes against much of the received wisdom I have played Test cricket under and for a group of players largely unchanged from the challenging few years we have just had, something is unlocked for everyone.

Baz's manner is the same regardless of the game's situation. Generally smiling and positive, he has a way of making players feel relaxed. Joe Root gets out reverse-scooping and Baz says to him, 'Good ball that, mate.' He follows this up with, 'Next time, hit it for six,' and his humour immediately puts everyone at ease. It's a mindset so far removed from the England team I joined almost 20 years ago that it makes the game seem almost unrecognisable.

Stokes's role is as key as Baz's. Right from the beginning, he leads from the front. He projects how the team should be playing – large, like a peacock, sometimes sacrificing his personal performance in order to lay down intent. After a day's play, Cooky, now a commentator, says to me in private, 'I think he's gone too far. It's too attacking.' But there is method in what he is doing. He is showing the way.

We play golf most afternoons after practice. Baz will say, 'Right, we finish at 12pm today because we have a tee time at 2pm.' It's an attitude once unthinkable for an England coach, but I feel like it might be another stroke of genius. No longer are we playing endless cricket for the sake of it, going down wormholes or negative spirals. The focus is on quality not quantity, priority given to players being fresh, both mentally and physically, rather than over-prepared.

There is no sleeping in the dressing room any more when we bat. Our batters are going at everything and, unbelievably, to begin with it pays off. Jonny Bairstow scores 136 in 92 balls, hunting down a total of 299 against New Zealand that many England teams would have not dared to chase. It is entertaining hitting that would not even be seen in most short form cricket games – pure theatre and exhilarating expression. From there, a catalyst is sparked. Jack Leach chases a ball to the boundary, diving head first, and injures himself in the process, yet Brendon McCullum tells him it's one of the best things he's ever seen and he should do it more often. People like Mark Wood thrive too – their super strengths celebrated and encouraged rather than over-analysed.

We follow this with a 3-0 series win in Pakistan, an unprecedented victory with our batsmen scoring at absurd rates. It seems to all fall out of the sky and work. When an airborne virus sweeps through the side and makes the entire team sick the day before the first Test, Stokes crawls to the door, opens it and shouts for Jack Leach next door, asking him to get a doctor. Everyone is very sick all night, before Stokesy texts the team in the morning saying, 'I'm up for it if you are.' Everyone agrees to play. We win the Test and become the first visiting team to win three matches in a series in Pakistan.

We start 2023 looking to continue this extraordinary run of results. It's the second Test in Wellington and we are batting last in a tight game. Where teams in the past would have batted to survive, this time we are trying to win. I am there, of course, trying to salvage something at the end. I hit Neil Wagner for four, meaning we only require two to win. He then bowls a bouncer that sails at least two metres over my head. I gesture at the umpires, but they don't call wide. I keep looking at them in disbelief, knowing what probably comes next. The next ball is at my body and I manage to get something on it, but I turn around to see the keeper take the catch. We have lost by a run. Unlike Sri Lanka though, I am not bent over, wanting the earth to swallow me up. We tried to win the game and we did everything we could to make a Test match entertaining. It's a consolation that surprisingly goes some way to healing the hurt I would have felt in the past. It's the kind of team I want to play in for another ten years, putting me half in mind to do a deal with a theoretical wizard. Just, whatever you do, don't call it 'Bazball'. Baz can't stand that phrase.

CHAPTER 54

END OF AN ERA

27–31 July 2023

ENGLAND vs AUSTRALIA, 5th Test, *The Oval, London*

England 283 and 395; Australia 295 and 334

England won by 49 runs

Australia 2nd innings: **S Broad 20.4–4–62–2**; Last wicket
A Carey c Bairstow b Broad 28

7–9 March 2024

INDIA vs ENGLAND, 5th Test, *H Pradesh CA Stadium, Dharamshala*

England 218 and 195; India 477

India won by an innings and 64 runs

India 1st innings: **J Anderson 16–2–60–2**

India 1st innings: **K Yadav c Foakes b Anderson 30**
(700th Test wicket)

Broady is the last of the old generation to go – retiring after the 2023 Ashes. It's a breathless series, the closest Ashes contest there has been for years, one that spins into all kinds of moralistic storylines and rhetoric over 'Bazball' and reaches fever pitch when Jonny Bairstow is stumped by Alex Carey, walking out of his crease thinking it's the end of the over. Just like Cooky, Broady plays his last Test at The Oval, with an ending he couldn't have written better if he'd tried.

A six with the last ball he faces, a wicket with the last ball he bowls, winning an Ashes Test for England for the last time and squaring the series. It's one of the most awe-inspiring, heroic things I've ever seen, complete with his bail-changing tricks and all the theatre he has learned to switch on at his will. It's the most glorious, unbelievable way to go. With the Oval already full to the last seat, we walk out to bat together on the first morning to a guard of honour from the Australians. I'm the first person he tells that he is retiring and just like Cooky, he says he wants to test the words in front of me to make sure it feels right. And still, I watch him leave and do not think of my own legacy moment or even that maybe I should do. I just think that I will play until I'm stopped. I will never end my own career for England.

It's an Ashes series that doesn't click personally, my best moment probably coming at the Major League Baseball London Series at the London Stadium where I zing a first pitch twice as hard as Nathan Lyon's before the St. Louis Cardinals take on the Chicago Cubs. But I give myself a talking to and get myself into the best shape I have ever been in my life for the India tour. I feel as strong as I've ever been, as enthusiastic about playing for England as ever, and at the foot of the Himalayas in

Dharamshala, become the first fast bowler ever to take 700 Test wickets. My dad is there to see it. I look up at the mountains as I leave the ground, unaware I will soon be walking into that Manchester hotel to be told I only have one game left. If I had the chance, I would have climbed that mountain again, the same way I did leaving Burnley, just to feel that thrill of belonging and the buzz of giving my service to something bigger than I could ever be.

CHAPTER 55

BACK ON THE BENCH

I am back on the bench. A raging hangover. An empty cricket field in front of me, the voice of a faceless man asking if I miss it that much already. As he leaves, I sit up slowly, the field and the pavilion coming into view – out of blurriness and back into focus. It is so still. Everything is so quiet. I feel like I have been running for a lifetime, all those collated incidents, all that drama and hurt and joy, all that noise and all those questions, to end up at the same spot. My whole universe has been inside that rope – my whole life held inside. It is the only space that promised it could hold me, take my imagination and offer it a place to exist, show me every corner of the globe, teach me that the world is as big as my life is small, and take that teenager and make him someone else.

I feel a sudden and profound sense of gratitude. I would happily bowl forever. It could be to all the tens of thousands yesterday that spilt across the playing field at Lord's, or to no one here. Just bowling a ball on a cricket pitch – the feeling of the seam leaving the fingers, knowing that it is exactly right as soon as it leaves the hand. The evolution of self, being able to trace my entire life back through one motion and action. The love of it will never leave me. Then I realise, maybe Jimmy and James, the two characters on and off the field that I was trying to reconcile and keep away from each other, were not two different people after all. It was all me – all the messy complexity of what a human is; I just lived it out under the eternal focus of an England cap. We would always talk about leaving that cap in a better place. I hope, looking out on to this empty pitch, that maybe I have left cricket in a better place too. If not the wickets, then at least with the dedication towards it – a love that is too pure, too unconditional, too deep to ever be put out.

I don't think I have ever seen a cricket pitch completely deserted from the outside before. Somehow it plays with my imagination, conjuring it to sketch out everything that has happened inside a boundary just like this for nearly 30 years. It's like I'm watching myself from outside now, every version of myself that has been and gone. I am there as a child, half the size of everyone else, throwing myself around in a bid to somehow make a telling contribution, before sulking my way back to the boundary when I haven't, head tucked into my chest, kicking the floor.

Then there are the magical moments in Burnley when bowling fast was suddenly gifted into my body, like a wish that I had been praying for so much from that solitary bench, and alone at night in bed, it had finally been granted. I'm bowling for Lancashire, being encouraged by all those heroes to run in as fast as I can, to not worry about anything else. I'm making my debut at the MCG, ill-fitting clothes hanging off me, no name on the back of my shirt. Then there's all the wickets in those early years, all those famous batters I had imagined to be superheroes just years before, turned inside out into S shapes, their stumps out of the ground.

Then the pain and the tears, the nerves, the searching and the over-thinking. The background changes in my mind – from Burnley to Lord's, Australia to South Africa, India to Pakistan – each setting changing in every way imaginable, the cricket inside still the same. I am there, holding the Ashes urn, at first once, then for a fourth time, before sitting on the outfield with each generation of teammates, our families too, sharing what happened, laughing into the fading light as we re-enact what we have just done.

With it all behind me, my career only a day old but somehow an ocean and a river between me and it now, I feel like I'm treading water in this unknown space. It's as if it all happened without effort, like it was always meant to. But I remind myself that every single day required effort. I don't want to forget the conscious energy it took to wake up and make the choice. To choose to try and improve, to choose to reach inside of myself, however painful, and find something that took me beyond where I had been before. I was always searching for that feeling, that perfection. As good as I got, I never reached it. There was always something else to find. That's why I would never have retired by my own decision. I could never turn my back on all that. The curiosity, the hunger, the love, could never be dimmed and, even the small moments it did briefly, it always returned stronger and brighter than it had ever been. I felt that even this time yesterday, bowling to the West Indies, chasing that inconsequential ball to the boundary as if my life depended on it. As the memories vanish back into the emptiness, I ask something of myself. It is like the cricketer I have been, the one I've just watched flash through his career, is speaking to the person I am becoming now. Always look for the hope that comes from the daily act of showing up. That is where the genius has always been. Remember that.

It strikes me as I look out on to the pitch, contemplating whether I miss it that much already, that my life now will be this exact view: the outside looking in. This is how I will experience cricket now – from this vantage point. It's like I'm looking at it for the first time. Just as I have learned again and again, cricket is good at renewal, at gifting transformation. I don't know what the future will be. It could all be brand new.

ACKNOWLEDGEMENTS

JIMMY

I want to thank everyone who has played a part in my career: coaches, captains and teammates. I've met some amazing people and made some great friends. Thanks for helping make the journey unforgettable.

Physios and doctors – the unsung heroes – thank you for keeping me on the field for the best part of 20 years.

The fans – England is the best supported team in cricket. On long tours, the travelling support always kept me going.

My mum and dad. Thanks for encouraging me to play sport and helping grow my love for it. Thanks also to my uncles and grandads for shipping me round to cricket clubs across the North West and beyond.

Daniella, Lola and Ruby – there is no way I would have achieved what I have without you. Thank you for your unwavering support and being my biggest fans. I love you, x.

Finally, thank you to the many people who had a hand in this book and helped me put my journey into words. The team at Bonnier for their support, and of course to Felix, who articulated a lifetime more eloquently than I ever could.

FELIX

Firstly, a huge thank you to Daniella Anderson for sharing such personal things in her own life so eloquently, which really helped make this book what it is. Some other very important people lent a lot of time and spoke in depth too: Catherine and Michael Anderson, Sarah Mackie, Joe Root, Alastair Cook, Stuart Broad, Mike Watkinson, Mark Bawden, Gaz Halley and Dave Brown.

The following people heard ideas, read drafts of chapters and/ or lent valuable encouragement throughout – Greg James, Matt 'Mattchin Tendulkar' Horan, Mark 'Sharky' Sharman, Barney Douglas, Tamzin Merchant, Steve Williams, Hattie Williams, Craig Brown and Florence Welch.

My agent, Nick Walters, has been great throughout the process. Thank you to him and David and everyone at David Luxton Associates – they all really, sincerely love cricket, which helps. Matt Phillips, Joe Hallsworth and Saira Nabi at Bonnier have been absolutely brilliant in their almost-daily interaction and support with the writing. Special thanks to Matt for his clarity of vision and helping me find a stronger, sharper sense of what we were trying to achieve.

My grandad – Harry Odell – passed cricket on to me with endless time and enthusiasm and love. He would have been genuinely amazed that I had written the story of England's greatest ever cricketer with him. My part in this book is for him.

Finally, and most of all, thanks to Jimmy for everything he has given to cricket and for the inspiration and effect he has had on my life, from a fan to a friend.

INDEX